# AFTERLIFE

**Polly Clark** was born in Canada and brought up in Scotland. She received an Eric Gregory Award for her poetry in 1997. Three collections followed from Bloodaxe: the first, *Kiss* (2000), was a Poetry Book Society Recommendation; her second, *Take Me with You* (2005), was a Poetry Book Society Choice and shortlisted for the T.S. Eliot Prize; her third was *Farewell My Lovely* (2009). Her pamphlet, A *Handbook for the Afterlife* (Templar, 2015), was shortlisted in the 2016 Michael Marks Awards. Poems from these collections and new poems are included in *Afterlife: New & Selected Poems* (Bloodaxe Books, 2026).

Her debut novel, *Larchfield* (Quercus, 2017), fictionalised a little-known period in the life of W.H. Auden. It won the *Mslexia* Prize, as well as critical plaudits from Margaret Atwood, Louis de Bernières and Richard Ford. It was featured in the BBC television documentary *Stop All The Clocks*, about W.H. Auden's life. Her follow-up, *Tiger* (Quercus, 2019), was shortlisted for the Saltire Scottish Book of the Year. Her third novel, *Ocean*, was published by Eye Books in 2025. Polly Clark's essays and journalism have been published in *The Guardian*, *The Scotsman*, *The Observer* and *The Financial Times*, and on her Substack, *Monday Night Reads*. Her poetry has been widely broadcast on BBC radio.

Polly Clark divides her time between the west of Scotland and a houseboat in London.

# POLLY CLARK

# Afterlife

NEW & SELECTED POEMS

BLOODAXE BOOKS

Copyright © Polly Clark 2000, 2005, 2009, 2015, 2026

ISBN: 978 1 78037 372 0

First published 2026 by
Bloodaxe Books Ltd,
Eastburn,
South Park,
Hexham,
Northumberland NE46 1BS.

www.bloodaxebooks.com
For further information about Bloodaxe titles
please visit our website and join our mailing list
or write to the above address for a catalogue.

LEGAL NOTICE
All rights reserved. No part of this book may be
reproduced, stored in a retrieval system, or
transmitted in any form, or by any means, electronic,
mechanical, photocopying, recording or otherwise,
without prior written permission from Bloodaxe Books Ltd.

Requests to publish work from this book
must be sent to Bloodaxe Books Ltd.

Polly Clark has asserted her right under
Section 77 of the Copyright, Designs and Patents Act 1988
to be identified as the author of this work.

Cover design: Neil Astley & Pamela Robertson-Pearce.

Printed in Great Britain by Bell & Bain Limited, 303 Burnfield Road,
Thornliebank, Glasgow G46 7UQ, Scotland, on acid-free paper
sourced from mills with FSC chain of custody certification.

*For Julian*
*who loved my poems from the beginning*

# ACKNOWLEDGEMENTS

This selection has been made by Polly Clark, with new or previously uncollected poems now comprising a new collection, *Afterlife*, followed by her selections from her previous three books published by Bloodaxe Books: *Kiss* (2000), *Take Me with You* (2005) and *Farewell My Lovely* (2009).

Thanks are due to the editors of the following publications in which poems or earlier versions of poems in the *Afterlife* section first appeared: *The Dark Horse*, *Magma*, *1914: Poetry Remembers*, ed. Carol Ann Duffy (Faber and Faber, 2014), *Ploughshares* (USA), *Poetry London* and *The Poetry Review*. 'My Mother's Hands' was a finalist in the *Mslexia* poetry competition 2024. 'Birdsong' was shortlisted for the 2025 Bridport Poetry Prize. Eleven of these poems were included in a pamphlet, *A Handbook for the Afterlife* (Templar, 2015), shortlisted for the 2016 Michael Marks Award.

Acknowledgements are due to the soldiers and officers of the Falklands War whose accounts of the conflict inspired the sequence *I Thought It Was in Scotland*.

# CONTENTS

**Afterlife** (2026)

| | |
|---|---|
| 15 | Sculpture |
| 16 | Muse |
| 18 | Birdsong |
| 20 | Paella Night |
| 21 | Heaven |
| 22 | That night a storm |
| 24 | Men |
| 25 | Seawanhaka Yacht Club |
| 26 | Io |
| 27 | Highland Cow |
| 28 | How to be a Poet |
| 29 | Handbook |
| 30 | Drain |
| 32 | The Woman Zoo |
| 33 | Hive |
| 34 | Port Meadow |
| 35 | The Crowded Earth |
| 36 | Interrogation |
| 37 | Crossing |
| 38 | Graduation Photo, 1964 |
| 39 | The Mermaid |
| 40 | Follower |
| 42 | The Pet Man |
| 43 | Her Kind |
| 44 | My Mother's Hands |
| 45 | Fire Starter |
| 46 | Spell |
| 48 | Pelican |
| 49 | Whale |
| 50 | Tiger, Tiger |

*from* **Kiss** (2000)

55 Love Story
56 Snow
57 Letter from Pécs
58 Road to Chisholm
59 Brief Encounter
60 Adultery
61 Retribution
62 Zoo
64 When You Were Made
65 In the Pool Room
66 Pilgrimage
67 South Uist
68 Where Swans Have Lain Down
69 If You're Interested
70 Last Tango in the Men's Department
71 My Life with Horses
72 A Lunch Date with My Father
73 Take-off
74 My Mother Marries My Father
75 When I Close my Eyes
76 Flowers
77 Excitement
78 New Forest Ponies
79 Walk in the Rain
80 Sunset
81 Amsterdam
82 Szechèny Tér
82   I *The Consultant*
83   II *The Angels*
84   III *The Wish*
85   IV *The Dream*
86 Szalon Sör
87 How to Love You
88 Stephen Selects the Photographs
90 Letter to the Man I Love

| | |
|---|---|
| 92 | Casualty Report |
| 93 | Crime of Passion |
| 94 | My Education at the Zoo |
| 96 | Dora |
| 98 | Baby |
| 99 | The Pet Rabbit |
| 100 | The Walk of Faith |
| 102 | Dear Virginia Ironside |
| 103 | The Writing on the Fridge |
| 104 | Bears |
| 106 | Pilate Comes to My Father's Deathbed |
| 108 | Progress Diary |
| 109 | Metamorphosis |
| 110 | Kleptomaniac |
| 111 | My Faithless Mouth |

*from* **Take Me with You** (2005)

| | |
|---|---|
| 115 | The Poetry God |
| 116 | My Life, the Sea |
| 117 | The Voyage of the Rays |
| 118 | Swan |
| 119 | Fishing Boat |
| 120 | Hedgehog |
| 121 | Elvis the Performing Octopus |
| 122 | Nibbling |
| 123 | Buffalo Mozzarella |
| 124 | Baize |
| 125 | The Lexicographer Finishes P |
| 126 | Nagyvázsony Castle |
| 127 | Proposal from the Bottle Bank |
| 128 | My Husband |
| 129 | Dumbarton |
| 130 | Your Wife |
| 132 | Mule |
| 133 | Women |

| | |
|---|---|
| 134 | Two Views of Loch Long |
| 134 | I *Dance* |
| 135 | II *Lost Property* |
| 136 | Two Views of a Submarine |
| 138 | Still Life with Table and Loch |
| 139 | Wave |
| 140 | Fairytale |
| 141 | Defenestration |
| 142 | Desiderata |
| 143 | Domestic Science |
| 144 | Rainbow |
| 145 | XX |
| 146 | My America |
| 147 | Beijing |
| 148 | Chengdu Massage |
| 149 | Flights Over Siberia |
| 150 | Bride |

*from* **Farewell My Lovely** (2009)

### *I Thought It Was in Scotland:*
A FALKLANDS WAR STORY

| | |
|---|---|
| 155 | Landing |
| 156 | Not a Crap Hat |
| 157 | May Your God Go with You |
| 158 | Wild Horses |
| 159 | Dear Mum |
| 160 | Bruce Lee at Goose Green |
| 161 | Fame! |
| 165 | Bay Tree |
| 166 | You Would Drop Your Spade |
| 167 | Tour of Landscapes by the Artist |
| 168 | Bar Harbor, Maine |
| 169 | Shoes |
| 170 | Yariguies Brush Finch |
| 171 | Marriage |
| 172 | Disorder |

| | |
|---|---|
| 173 | Farewell My Lovely |
| 174 | Dressed Up As Someone |
| 175 | Islay |
| 176 | Little Black Dog |
| 177 | Dog Opera |
| 178 | Trash |
| 179 | Our Baby |
| 180 | Laparoscopy |
| 181 | Moon |
| 182 | Return to Eden |
| 183 | Magnificat |
| 184 | Beheaded |
| 185 | Special Care Unit |
| 186 | She |
| 187 | Ladies |
| 188 | Directions |
| 189 | The First Woman |
| 190 | Friends |
| 191 | Smile |
| 192 | Another Girl |
| 193 | The Book of Truths |
| 194 | Struck |
| 197 | Baby Group |
| 198 | A Bench for Me |
| 199 | Soup |
| 200 | Sex in the City |
| 201 | Last Will and Testament |
| 202 | Thank You |
| 203 | Advice to a Daughter |
| 204 | To My Husband |
| 205 | Tell Laura I Love Her |

# Afterlife

(2026)

# Sculpture

Michelangelo to this lump
of cold relationship, I persist
without commission, chipping
for years at life-shortening angles.
But I am satisfied by your eyes.
*David* has love hearts for pupils.
I bring your eyes to life with ink.
How perfect are your arms
as you lean over to break the news –
can I hold you there forever,
like *David* in the moment before battle?
Perhaps there should be no pupils at all.
Considering this makes me giddy.
A pretty dog sleeps at the neighbouring table.
I include it. The sculptor's little joke.
Later, in Trafalgar Square, when it is time,
you slide your arms around me
burying your face in my neck
and I get to work inside the warmth
of your living marble. The sky
is swirling, as happens in the city.
How beautifully we slot together,
not lip to lip but cheek to cheek, body to body.
For years in the studio, I will carve this moment,
over and over, though you have forgotten me.
We are living, somewhere, deep in this work.
It's what I'm made for, though I longed for more.

# Muse

His lubricious way of turning the page, eyeing me.
*This line is wonderful*, he said.
*But here –*
*and by* here, *I mean* you *– toe-curlingly awful.*

He bowed, a pied-piper –
                my words trotted after him, urchins, piglets.
We were out of control.
He ate my heart for breakfast, lunch, dinner.
He unhinged his jaw like a snake and swallowed it whole.

I loved that.
It didn't hurt at all.

When he felt formal,
he sliced my heart into petals using a silver knife.
*Be dead, like me*, he was saying.

I'm really trying to, I said,
stubbornly enjoying my chips, ordering wine at his expense.

When I gave him a little of what he wanted –
cried, quadruple texted him,
fucked a sailor and told him the details –
he smiled, beckoned me closer,
then swung – hard.

He denied it, of course.

He ate my feminism as a morning snack,
snapped it like a pretzel before my bowed head.

I wrote him a poem in protest.
He betrayed me to the authorities.

I said to them: *how shall I live?*
*He's turned my blood into a private language.*

They put me on hold.
*Pavane Op. 50* played seven times.

A voice came back:
*Sorry,*
*there's no one of that name here.*

# Birdsong

In those middle years I was so hungry,
for pasta, fat pats of butter on rye,
soft, fleshy sponges, New York cheesecake.
I was ravenous like a caterpillar on a leaf.
If I chomped and chomped would I get back
to a unified something that was me?
No one knew I was hungry like that.
I gulped down air and looked extraordinary.
In the city, the exhausts were singing.
People were taller than in the past.
On our plates were piled slivers of things.
Everything was divided and divided again
until whole things no longer existed.
Almost a century after we split the atom,
we split a word from its meaning.
From then on, the air glittered dangerously.
We wiped meaning, like an insult, from our lips.
Words were kind; meaning was treason.
I was afraid to describe my hunger.
I hoarded meanings like tins under the stairs,
licking and nibbling them when I was alone.
I longed to share them with someone,
but *Protect and Survive* said no.
Planes flew overhead, always at the same angle.
I thought about my father. He followed me
all my life, even when he was dead,
becoming man after man, staying as that man
until he'd eaten me up, then moving on.
From father to daughter passes the hunger.
I gorged in the shadows like a snake.
I was so hungry I could not trust myself.
If I could just be satisfied I would be beautiful.
I shed so many skins and hid them all –

people would think I was a serial killer
when I was just outgrowing myself.
To thrive, I grew stiff, a Russian doll.
The tiniest one inside was so hungry
you could hear her crying to be free.
I opened my mouth and out flew birdsong,
meaningless, inedible, lovely.

## Paella Night

How it bubbles in the centre of the room
like a sun we're going to get to eat.
Diego arranges the langoustines

in a worshipful circle, eyes to the centre.
We're deep in a mother's home.
I am so happy to write about paella.

The women are tired and beautiful
in their soft blouses, sipping their Cava.
This is the reception for the afterlife

when I meet my fellow ghosts.
How young we are in our mother's clothes.
We giggle and whisper how we got here.

## Heaven

is the place we'll go to when we die
and we'll all be together. Hamish too,
though yes, on a lead. At 5 p.m. over cheesy pasta
the matter of the afterlife has to be solved.
Officially there now is an afterlife; absolutely
empirically, definitively, because my daughter
is broken-hearted that we will die and leave her
without mummy and daddy. I won't have it.
My child's happiness will not be sacrificed
to the rational ideology of dust. In short –
we have brought it back. We talk into the night
you and I, planning the detail of the place
we'll all go to be together. We come alive;
for one-night-only we're God, dividing
the dark from the light and making it good.
I want to wake her from the deep teary
slumber she's fallen into to tell her, darling
it has a name, the place we're all going to
with Hamish on a lead, it has a lovely name.
Daddy and I forgot to tell you, here, I'll whisper –
everyone you love will be there.

## That night a storm

broke over my boat.
The mooring lines groaned.

My canvas ceiling shook
like an ocean of cormorants,

capes open to freezing north.
I felt my heart breaking.

I felt its ragged edges
when I pressed my sternum.

Dawn lay soft upon the river
as I lifted out my heart

and set it free upon the water
like Moses in his basket.

I sank into my mud-soft bed,
curling like an ammonite

in a time before commandments.
No god loved or punished me.

I drifted beyond prophecy,
down into formlessness.

And there, I mastered
the art of separation:

darkness from light. Honour
from dishonour. I became

prime mover of my loss of you.
Last, I made a tiny moon.

I clutched it to my empty chest,
breathed upon it, delighted

by its icy possibilities,
my newborn, stony life.

# Men

After some years in the seaside town,
she began to see men everywhere.
Their awed faces gasped in the waves.
It was clear they were not drowning,
even as the sea climbed up
and dashed them on the winding road.
Some of them were men she knew:
her friend's husband, the lawyer,
turned in the hollow of a wave;
she saw old lovers and nearly lovers,
and men she never liked,
and men she'd seen on the Tube.
The dead ones weren't dead any more.
Some were little boys, their fingers made
the wiggly crests of each wave.
And now, when she left the shore,
the grass was men, the trees were men,
Men were pressed into the walls
of the little house she loved so.
They spoke to her, of course they did,
inviting her to press against them,
to stretch beneath them,
to meet with her lips
the freezing gravity of them.

# Seawanhaka Yacht Club
*Long Island*


I should like to stay here and never die,
sail forever these golden waters.

Dawn strides over the lawn like an award.
Today I shall not burn, unless I forget my hat,

and if I do, Joe will lend me his and I shall be saved.
He will carry me across the water in his cruiser.

We will follow my daughter racing in her sonar,
so I can photograph her breaking free, her beautiful hair like birds.

The sea is singing in its bonds.
Reaching for his arm, strong as a mast,

I whisper, *I don't know how to love her, Joe.*
He is warm and dry; it is right to cling to him.

But he is only a loyal boatman.
He cannot take me where she goes.

At the setting of the sun
we gather on the shore and sing

as the Stars and Stripes is lowered
and rolled tenderly, like baby clothes.

I remember loving her like that,
my heart a ricochet across the sound.

# Io

I am the second-smallest
but your innermost.
I am careful, always my same face
to you, though I cannot help

my incandescent blush,
my flash of wickedness,
the green tide of my longing
for you, my unreachable

love. My orbit has a tiny
eccentricity, a tweak on perfection,
like a gap tooth, a funny gait,
not beautiful, but singular.

Your need flexes inside me.
Mine is the most restless
body in the solar system.
I lost my water and my ice,

the price of being close to you.
But in turn, you can't escape
my face, its changing questions.
I breathe out fiery mountains.

I breathe them in again.
I am so lonely, Jupiter.
The pull of your jealousy
swings us in endless resonance.

We are *how things are*.
Even Galileo saw my bondage;
your unrelenting want
that holds me burning always.

# Highland Cow

And there she was,
as if she had stepped, casually,
out of the pasture of my body
(like the wire fence trodden on the grass
where I pass each day, where the farmer
has given up against the sheep, the deer,
the night creatures who need to get somewhere).
She slapped her nose with her fat pink tongue
sank her hairy thighs in the pool,
while the sun burned around her
and the mountains fidgeted in silence.
The flies that walk on water gathered round her
and the swallows upended and soared on their backs
because there is something like the end
of your life's pilgrimage to see a beast
so whole and finished and strange.
I wiped my eyes (it's what I do these days
instead of setting off at a stomp for the past)
and she lifted her lump of a head,
water dripping from her lips,
as if to say, *why not follow me?*
*In me you shall find peace, in me you shall find how*
*to be in the wrong world, with majesty, forever.*

## How to be a Poet

Appeasement is my genius. It needs only
excision of memory; an amputated story.
When I was born I stepped on a mine.
It blew my history away. Left glitter

and scraps I discovered behind things:
fairy tales, rooms of coffee-ringed paper.
I collated them all with great panache,
waved them to show peace for our time.

# Handbook

In the afterlife your loved ones
will fail to see you. Your shadow

will cling to others, confusing them.
Your words will sound like theirs.

This is a downside of the afterlife,
not fully dealt with in the handbook.

We should put it in somewhere.
We never quite get around to it

I suppose imagining that you know
how lucky you are to be here.

Now we're on the subject,
the other thing not quite expanded on

apart from the searing damp
and that your favourite colour won't exist

is that a small girl will follow you
to the ends of the earth.

It is of course your animated bones
that she follows, but still.

Who needs that grief anyway?
Who cares about who you were?

# Drain

He splashes up the drive, rods in hand,
a cowboy in overalls from another time.
He's the only game in town, so it's been two weeks
of hopeful calls, and years of Christmas gifts.
He hates these clay runes laid down centuries ago,
wishes everything was plastic and nothing
was underground. He's brought his hose,
a plunger and a pickaxe. His face is composed:
sadness for the failure of character which has brought
this blockage upon us. We welcome him with tea and Marigolds
but he shakes his head. *My uncle said all gloves
are for poofters.* And thus begins our journey
into the bowels of this weary house. He's got the toilet
off its base – *fucked I'm afraid* – leaving
its neck raw and slender as Mary Queen of Scots's;
then he's feeding – yard by yard – thirty feet of rods
down the hole, thrusting and groaning in a weird pornography.
*It's no good, we'll have to dig up the pipe.
I hate digging up pipes.* Out he goes, and the axe
crunches mournfully – what can be down there?
*I've not seen a choke like this for years,* he wails:
*we'll have to saw the pipe.* The saw whines
and down goes the hose, and on goes the tap,
and round the corner we've got the drain lid off,
waiting like expectant parents, will this be it?
He lumbers round to look, and suddenly *Och! No!*
something gives, something lets go, we feel it,
a great clot of disgust, of stuff that didn't go to hell,
here it comes, vast gobs of brown sludge, sanitary towels
*(a guest, Mrs Forrester, I know you wouldn't do that),*
foam, shiny things, miraculously preserved toilet paper:
the procession of our worst goes on for ages
and we stand till it's completely gone, and dark is falling

and he stands with us, smoking and shaking his head
and chatting with my husband about the old folk,
how they buried Miss Tavistock yesterday,
how she used to take him sailing when he was a wee lad.

## The Woman Zoo

We're as common as the improbable fold and
        fold again of the sea's grey hide;
common as muck, with its guts of ochre, that clings
        to your tyres, your boots, your fingers.
See our flanks anytime, without binoculars, stamping,
        primordial. You need only demand,
or spy us in our reservation, coughing in a haze
        of ginger steam and Dulux Savannah.
We lumber from room to room, from year to year,
        dumb, slightly drunk with amazement.
We woke up in a world we don't recognise, that's all,
        that watches patiently, like extinction.
On the radio today, the urgent call for conservation.
        We say nothing, chase the birds
into the sky, then turn back to our patch of lawn.
        Observe us snort, breed, weep.
We know everything there is to know about survival.

# Hive

Fattened bees drag themselves
in perfect diagonals
towards the margin of the door.

Not a single one makes it.
Each dawn I lift the waving forms.
And who shall save me?

Shall it be the irritable wives
busy in their kitchens?
The husbands who smell of honey?

The Community? Disney? God?
My neighbour's words dance and thrum:
> *I don't know what my purpose is*

I longed to grab her hand and ask,
Your husband? Mine? Our children?
                              Love?

Perhaps the garden holds the answer,
sleepy with its nectars.
It's where I dig and clip and hum.

Oh my neighbour, are we safe?
Is this what being safe
is like?

## Port Meadow

Creeping buttercup, weedy cousin
of proper buttercup fills Port Meadow

and if you sit there in the high summer,
petals to the horizon and to your waist

it is like waking on the battlefield,
but afterwards, in the promised heaven.

I have the buttercups in a frame on my desk,
a photo from that day. All their heads

point the same way, off-camera,
to a white tunnel of inescapable grace.

# The Crowded Earth
(After Vera Brittain, *A Testament of Youth*)


A million friends have flipped their backs,
words blown off and limbs vestigial.
His hands are bent against his waist
like fins in the petrified sea, as he sinks
towards a beginning neither he nor I believed in:
the instant, the flash, the bang.

I do not cry. As I open my door into snow
a woman jostles me, walks on. Words are smithereens
and beyond my skills to mend. Life is stripped
to the letter, the N...N...N of loneliness
the V...V...V of love. Friends turn to hide
their tearless faces and I do the same.

In my nurse's uniform I swim among fresh
failures of the broken earth. They flail
and moan as if born today, unwillingly.
Most soon drift to the sea-bed, their little fins curled.
A few – not him – we drag to the surface, and teach
to move among us, their eyes bright and glazed.

## Interrogation

The sun's a searchlight.
The sky turns it into my eyes.

Everything under the sun
is either living or dead.

So… *what's it to be?*
The climate's made extremists of us all.

My eyelids are burning.
I lick my lips.

I whisper,
The object of my love is gone

but the love remains.
I've told you everything I know.

# Crossing

It looks like a pleasure trip
but I've got the heebie-jeebies.
My husband and daughter tut tut,
tell me not to be so silly.
My daughter puts her arms around me,
momentarily nails me to the earth
then sets me free. My husband
looks at me sadly, but full of love.
The boat has a little wooden slat to sit on
like the rowing boats we took in Oxford long ago.
The mist slips down around us, just me
and the boatman, who reminds me
of our old plumber from I forget where;
(he died and was resurrected,
and this man has the gentle set
of that man's jaw, his tired eyes).
Neither shore can be seen now:
it is just me and the man
who looks like another man.
I say to him, will I be gone long?
But replies are not what you get
in the boat from one shore to another.
Water clings in tiny fingertips to the oars,
falling with reluctance
like a child letting go to sleep.
The boatman reminds me of someone –
my father? That guy who won Euromillions?
I take off my glasses and wipe the drops
and notice that there is no difference.
The boatman smiles at that.
His shirt is soft cotton, his chest hair
curls with a touch of grey into its V.
*Loss is just the crossing.*
There's nothing for me now, but bliss.

# Graduation Photo, 1964

You've got to hand it to her, she's determined.
        Day after day in the photo on my desk
my mother smiles like the world's first teenager,
           her plump hands crossed across her tummy.

           Night after night after night
I unfold letters, and this girl
                    tumbles out.
She doesn't know the 60s have arrived.
She doesn't know they're happening to her.
She doesn't know she'll be shaking them
           out of her children forever.

Mother, the first in the family to go to university,
        the first woman with easy access contraception,
why did you lie there as if the future was far away,
        smiling, smokey-eyed, like a girl in a photo

                to which a man
with his fashionable sideburns and long cigarette
applies a match, just to see what will happen,
because he can, because he's curious,
because destruction, not progress, is in his heart.

# The Mermaid
*A Fairytale*

Once upon a time a mermaid saved two girls.
There they were in the swell,
their faces like spots of sun on the water.
One was screaming,

her blonde hair bobbing like seaweed,
her pink dress clinging like rain to a window.
The mermaid dragged them to shore by the hair.
They would have died without her violence.

The mermaid did not look back at the sea.
As she reached the beach she stumbled.
She gasped as she pulled herself upright
because to walk on a mermaid tail is agony.

The children stopped screaming.
On land they looked like sodden flowers.
She dragged them on regardless,
across the endless burning sand.

# Follower

Lately, I've been thinking about her a lot.
It's not just home and the office and the train
and the shops and mealtimes and the school gate
but in my dreams, day and night, and my stories
and now here.

I've been reading furiously,
searching for an answer to being followed,
how to control the situation, introduce visiting hours.
I thought it was perhaps just what happens
when you are a mother, but she never speaks,
nor cries, nor laughs. She's just there,
in her glasses, with her unkempt hair,
and the school uniform she slept in.

It's been 40 years. It's time.
I turn from the chair by the window
where the room faces directly into the past
and I beckon her onto my lap and she trots over
without any anger that she's been ignored all these years
and she climbs onto me careful not to disturb my clothes.

She asks for nothing. I slip my arms around her.
She has a tiny bald patch hidden by her tangled hair
and the side of her glasses has a metal grip:
they're the NHS pink ones circa 1976.
She smiles and she's missing a tooth,
and freckles sprinkle her pale cheeks.
Now is the moment to say something.
It's going to be so important for the future.

I hold her and drink in the abandoned smell of her,
and it's like at the animal shelter when the dog who asked nothing,
who sat quietly with its despair somehow did not merit
an end to it, but somehow earned more of the same.
The child and I sit as the afternoon yellows and crumbles,
and she is so patient that I fear for my mind, but at last
she slips down from my lap and goes to find her ladybirds.

## The Pet Man

My mother had a pet man.
She knitted him jumpers in the early 60s.
She wrote to his mother about his health.
She discussed his diet, his worries about science.
She married him, because it was good for him.
She developed a new language to talk about him.
Every sentence began with David, or He.
She wrote to his mother to ask for money.
The pet man was not very solvent
but seemed to like his treatment.
He wrote to his mother: 'This is the closest
I've come to understanding this marriage lark.'

In the late 60s, the pet man turned.
It was a different time, of liberation.
Losing her man changed my mother.
She did not write to his mother again.
She did not knit.
She said nothing about it,
except *don't do it. Don't do any of it.*
We understood an important lesson
was taking place. We listened at the door
of her bedroom as she chewed and spat,
emerged each morning bone-clean,
dressed and walking perfectly on two legs.

# Her Kind

My urchin eyes follow
as you say, *I hope she burns in Hell.*
My heart's a Ford Capri, you see.
My favourite colour's tight white.

I know two obscenities:
you can make good from nowt &
a council house is bigger than a Barratt
& is a good buy.

I'm the grubby child of Thatcher
who has nowhere to go back to.
My gloomy corner of the north
was swept away for good:

my granddad whistling
for his wife like a dog;
the ragged Blackpool sea,
its chain of donkeys clinking

like a distant arcade game.
Sometimes I listen for her,
as if to a conch. I dream of her –
the rustling dress of easy cash,

the incantation: *self-reliance, family.*
I miss my awkward, hungry kind
with our hard comeuppances,
our spines made of yellow brick road.

## My Mother's Hands

were neatly crossed, like the Queen's on TV.
She wore an expression of nothing

you could put your finger on, perhaps
the same tremulous freeze of Parkinson's

that my grandmother had in her last years
that made her appear composed and aloof

while I polished her nails in the nursing home
(then a tear would leak out and she'd pull away,

say *that's enough now*, slide one hand
into the freckled sheath of the other).

At Gran's funeral my mother's hand
slid towards mine where I sat beside her

on that hard front row with everyone missing.
I held it because I am her daughter.

It was not the hand with her old wedding ring –
the ring she tore off and threw at me –

but the other, with nails bitten raw.
My mother's face screwed up like a little girl's,

her hand in mine sweated and writhed.
And afterwards, it shed me like a skin,

recoiled to sculpted perfection,
preparing to touch no one ever again.

## Fire Starter

Match, firelighters, old drafts on dry paper –
these alone are not enough.
You must learn the language of *wet*:

has the wood been wept upon
or is it young and not for burning?
You must learn *season*, you must learn

to stack, to chop; you must long
to make it through the biting winter.
The sickly rot, the slime of too-late,

the scuttling shadows must not trouble you.
The flash of the axe, the way a log splits
like a neck, these may shock but you will do better

if the thud of log to floor is like a clock,
that soothes with its sameness and irregularity.
Most of all, you must learn the flame:

the creamy lick of the eternal;
the emberless chatter of the young;
the glow that promises rebirth with a touch.

## Spell

First, you must open the folder
where you put all his emails
and study those early ones.

Feel them beam, as they did then,
from him to you, bearing
something stolen,

now miraculously returning.
You must delete them all,
except those that breathe,

the ones that make you gasp,
because nothing was ever ended
without suffering somewhere, for someone.

These you must print off
and while your family go about
all the happy business that does not concern you –

because you are a ghost until you have done this –
light the stove with them
and feed it with your poems.

Make sure that the fire
roars before you close the door.
Now walk to where your phone lies.

You will be a person again.
You have not been a person for some time.
Your whole life, perhaps.

Scroll through your contacts
and when you reach his name
wipe it away with all his texts.

I wish I could tell you it was over now,
but this poem, this instruction,
preserves your ability to love.

It must be destroyed also.
Nothing must remain.
You must be clean as a fire,

new as a piece of paper.
Then and only then
can you be finished.

# Pelican

*St James's Park, London*

My love for you
gulps. It is dinosaurish,
profoundly unEnglish.
Oh my love's great beak
bends my neck upon my back.
My entire brain is a hinge
for my love for you.
And when my love flies,
the man on his lunchbreak
making a call on his birthday
can't believe his eyes. *Nan!* he cries,
*I thought their wings were clipped!*
My love for you is the star of the park,
landing in a clumsy splash –
slap! slap! go my love's pink feet,
right up to you, the one I've chosen.

# Whale

I lived my youth without constraint,
and the fish adored me for it.
Sardines, man o' wars, and all between

followed me as I metamorphosed
from spray into stars,
emptying my lungs of everything stale.

Shouldering waves in all their tonnage,
I left the fish agape, arcing the sun,
like a planet shining with life.

But outrage greeted me
when I became a blue full-grown.
The fish adored me no longer.

Sovereign among multitudes,
they despised my tales of dark and light,
my celestial respiration.

You can't have it all, they said.
You must choose –
Be fish with us, or breathe alone.

They scattered when I opened wide,
the ocean rushing in like sky.
Ascending, I embraced my life.

# Tiger, Tiger
*A Fairytale*

Once upon a time a girl ran away to join the zoo.
She was only herself in the company of animals.
Their smell and their wordlessness drew her.
Their silence was not a lack, but a better dimension.

At the zoo was a tiger, untamed and deadly.
She'd killed a keeper and only one man could manage her.
The girl stood at the tiger's glass when the visitors left,
when the keepers had gone, when only the strange hoots and howls
of a distilled animal world filled the night.
At these times the tiger was gentle.
She spoke from inside her cage,
words that only the girl could understand.
The tiger spoke about being trapped.
The tiger spoke about isolation.
Night after night the girl sat by the glass.

Meanwhile the girl fell in love with the tiger keeper.
He went to Greece on his holidays and mixed small letters
and capitals. He talked about fucking and bloody this and that.
With the tiger he was detached and respectful.
He expected that when she had a cub she would kill it.
He was lean and strong, and lazy like a cat.
One night the tiger keeper went home with the girl.

**Humiliate:** to lower or hurt the dignity or pride of.
**Virgin:** a person, esp. a woman who has never had sexual intercourse. Any female animal who has never mated. Not yet cultivated explored, exploited etc. by man. Occurring naturally in a pure and uncombined form.
**Pain:** the sensation of acute physical hurt or discomfort caused by injury, illness etc. Emotional suffering or distress. Punishment, grief.
**Painful:** causing pain: a painful duty. Extremely bad.

**Cruel:** causing or inflicting pain without pity.
**Crush:** to press, mash or squeeze so as to injure, break, crease etc. To break or grind into small particles. To put down or subdue esp by force. To extract (juice, water etc) by pressing. To oppress harshly. To hug or clasp tightly. To defeat or humiliate utterly as in argument or by cruel remark. To become injured, broken or distorted by pressure.
**Fear:** a feeling of distress, apprehension, or alarm caused by impending danger, pain etc. Awe, reverence, Fear of God. To be afraid (to do something) or of a person (or thing). To revere, respect. To be sorry.
**Grief:** deep or intense sorrow, esp at the death of someone.

And in that moment the soul of the girl and the soul of the tiger
each lifted from their body and the soul of the tiger
entered the body of the girl and the soul of the girl
entered the body of the tiger. And one story split into two stories,
for now the tiger could move and act in the world in the body of the girl,
and now the girl lived in the muscular confines of the tiger's body
with its daily respectful attention from the tiger keeper
and the lines of poems running through her head,
which she could think about from dawn until dawn.

But the tiger found that though she appeared free
her body was weak and no one was afraid.
She paced the boundaries of the zoo at night.
She listened to the keepers in their lodge
laughing and playing music. She was angry
but her body remained the girl's.
Her voice remained the girl's.

And the girl in the tiger's body lived like an anchoress,
and she grew to love her walls and bars,
and she worked out her poems in her great, beautiful head,
and from time to time she opened her eyes
and saw a girl standing in the shadow of the glass.

FROM
# Kiss
(2000)

## Love Story

You winked at me in the hospital chrome,
and turning in my sheets I found
the imprints of your lips and feet.
When darkness fell, the young girl opposite
was alone and began to cry,
I went to stroke her hair
and you returned to me, you were

the swarthy nurse in green
whose sole job was to lift girls
from bed to trolley and back again.
My arms around your neck,
I whispered, 'Nagyon erős',
it meant 'I love you', it meant don't leave me,
let me bury myself in your green cloth,
let me be such a clean thing.

And I saw you in the green waist
of my father, the surgeon, whose hand
reached from the sky to my face,
and said in a dream language,
*God is waiting at the door*
*and will go if you ask*. I watched
you leave me in the gleam of the needle
and I heard your pipe in the distance
and the anxious footsteps of daylight
pattering over me like children.

**Snow**

Your words are falling on me,
not one at a time, but in half-words,
in soft phrases, the exquisite *fizz!*
of a single letter on my tongue.
I walk home in a blizzard
of everything you have said to me;

and not only words, your touch
babbles warmly on my skin; syllable
by syllable you're obliterating
the dark needles of the fir trees; a crow
is trying to scythe himself free
of the fragments cohering
into one great white word.

# Letter from Pécs

This is my day: I put out milk for
the enormous winter-coloured tom,
who avalanches on my bed, out-staring me
with metal eyes, and I enclose your absence
in thick wool and a jacket,
running from my whitewashed cell into
the giant's windswept garden;

and now the nights are swallowing the mornings
as though the sun should never
have escaped at all; this winter everything
is sharpened: leaves and rooftops and
my breathing slicing
shapes out of the sky.

In a hole, somewhere, is a huge rusted key,
heavy with discovery by generations of children.
The tom knows where it is
(that's why I humour him), I think
he dragged it there, I think that everybody knows.
The gibbering people who inhabit this garden
will never tell me, sometimes I feel
I am a speck on their teeth, compressed
between their jolting lips, or
shivering on the whites of their eyes.

When my eyes open onto
this iron sheet of dawn, my heart
is dead and silver, frozen and beautiful like a snowflake.
When night opens its mouth
I throw it, high above the hunchbacked wall;
if you look tonight
you will see it, round and hoping,
looking for a place to fall.

## Road to Chisholm

Climbing the road to Chisholm, with
the mist weeping on the car, my grandmother
staring at a memory lost
in the verdant muddy verge, I saw
a galloping horse in the valley, orange
against the humbled green and the grey
mist-balls of sheep, galloping
calmly, like a film-horse.
We climbed until I almost saw
the stillness of its back.
No one saw it but me. No one spoke, not liking
to interrupt the steady command of the wipers
or fight the protests of the rain drawn
beneath the tyres. In this silence I followed it.
Who turned it loose in such a huge place,
who left it in the rain,
who knew what I knew, that love had left us,
and this was all we had,
the rain, our bodies, a destination.

# Brief Encounter

I never knew you, though
I wrote page upon page about
how you would feel inside my heart
and in my pen, and how
my life would be corrected
by the ballast of you in my gut. But
I never saw you, though I searched –
in the eye-whites of the gypsy, in
the smiles of people who never asked anything of me,
in traces of blood, flakes of skin,
one long curling hair which lay between
my pages. They all made words line up neatly in my mind,
but where were you? My authenticity,
the soul of everything I meant to say,
where were you, I never knew you.
Until today. I stood beneath the hot stream
of water, washing away my headache and hatred
for hour after hour, and then, in a drop on my eyelash,
I saw you move, I saw you move! I saw
your shiny black carapace
shrinking beneath hot tears of water
and your fat black legs
lumbering to safety. It was not what I imagined,
grief. Nor the convulsive reaction,
the terror, the urge to survive,
the roaring and stamping in my head,
the smell of heat and hallucinations, the voices,
bury the dead, bury the dead.

## Adultery

Water the plant every day, you say.
Taking it I cannot make our hands touch,

for I will still want you when you are old,
when memories and guilt make us cry,

when your loose-limbed frame of memories
bends its thin arms around me.

Our old old stories, we turn them over
like photos on the two-seater sofa;

the others sit quietly, strangely
tolerant of this love-making, this

non-contact of knees, averting of eyes,
banalities opened into like kisses.

We are numbed with shame, we converse
over and around it, the wordless please.

# Retribution

Snow, exploded stone,
a chance to be air
taken brutally –

coughing I raise myself,
wolf-backed, ape-handed,

like the girl I saw kicked to the floor,
who got up six times
and kept on walking,
eyes fixed beyond despair.

In my face
explodes the sky, expelling me;
unhappy excrement,
smother it, kick it,
the boy in boots has made his judgement.

The boy in boots
crashed his motorbike later,
impaled himself on railings.
I knew it was retribution.
I took his inarticulate hate
and made it my own.

## Zoo

I remember kicking the bales down
from the top of the barn, my eyes streaming.

The only creature I truly loved
hugged me, and I thought his animal warmth

was more wonderful than the touch on my cheek
from the gibbon with the circular brown eyes.

The orang-utan liked to scrub with a rag
and poke her leathery fingers through the bars,

and the elephant stood at the railings, curling
her trunk at the children,

her ears like rags, and her tusks
wrenched out; I thought

suffering must have a language, I loved
where love was wasted.

When the silly pop-eyed Père David
escaped across the zebras' frozen savannah

he chased it and threw
his great shoulders at its hooves

bringing it down in a trembling
thump, and I thought the breaking

of freedom was beautiful, I thought
I was discovering truth

in these limbs collapsing,
antlers falling against the sky,

and the snow in shreds
like a man's blue eye.

## When You Were Made

I think God was uncertain
when he dressed you in blue,

yanked your back up straight,
filled your eyes with ink,

made clumsy pens of your lips,
a blank page of your skin;

he was uncertain of your power,
could this bony thing, scribbling

poems and always alone
be a force to be reckoned with?

But still proud he sealed
your funny frame with a kiss,

carved you a perfect white shoulder
from Sirius.

## In the Pool Room

Under the lemony light,
my paw resting on the green baize,

his lion's mouth presses
a kiss like a roar into me.

Paws flounder into manes,
mouths break and seal,

and my throat bends like a belly,
while blue eyes blink in flat faces

and tails flicker round us.
Then it is over

like a shiver over sleeping ribs,
and I lick my lips,

like a young cub
digesting its first lesson.

## Pilgrimage

Across a clifftop stretched our shadows,
yours before you, mine behind you,

a pilgrimage over salty grass
to where the sun blazed the distant backs of seals.

The icy sea and track half-starved
whispered *it is never over*

and the overflowing sun
swept away my name.

We turned and saw a huge black dog
pound its way from a break in the earth,

to circle its master, barking.

# South Uist

In the morning the track paled
to fit only two feet pressing down
to the proud wreckage at the sea's breast.

All the long night I lay in your damp bed,
felt how the sheets that wrapped you
loved me less, breaking the hours

with sips of peat-treacled water.
I dreamed of you as dawn
flooded over the dry stone walls.

I never spoke of it. I broke instead
the bull's skull from its armoury of shells,
dragged it home, to bleach away its shadows.

## Where Swans Have Lain Down

Here where swans have lain down
lain down among the rushes,

like crinolines blown in the rushes
where light decays on the water,

leaving lines in fallen leaves
where flies unpunctuate the evening;

here where leaves like pages fall,
where ripples circle the drinking light,

a bird calls, clear as a name,
alone in the place where swans have lain down.

## If You're Interested

you're very talented my
favourites no girl
I ever knew before could
if you're interested
if you're interested
tarantino's women are all
running I'm getting a belly you'll
do brilliantly I'll see
you next week sometime shall I
break his legs for you? if you're
starving and I lost but I'm not
grumpy fantastic-looking
slim-wise, my favourites, if
you're easier to stop
now than later, if you're
sorry I'm trying to do the right
thing sorry I upset you sorry
I make you if you're interested
my favourites are running tonight

## Last Tango in the Men's Department

Shoulders stacked in cellophane,
pockets smell of hurt unborn,
of black, brown and blue,
the whirl of a bruise.

Mannequin girls tilt their heads
as they press the dark cashmere
hand to heart; I hold
the navy like a stranger I rescued,

beautiful creature,
I know the size of your shoe,
I know all about you,
how rooms sweep around you.

I spin as the lady
counts the rings of your neck,
your throat so close
she could scratch it or kiss it –

your trust is amazing,
but you can't hear the music:
the sadness of shoulders bent over knees,
the anger of metal lifted and swung,

the swirl of a dress
like a bloom blown in,
the break of the doors,
the thump of the sun.

## My Life with Horses

Before I knew there were men,
I galloped a pony bareback;
it was a hard winter, but
how sure-footed we were, resolute
in frozen emptiness, stamping
the ice with our names.

Years later I lay like a foal in the grass,
wanting to touch your hair;
we clutched like shadows,
I twined the past through my fingers, kissing
great gulps of father, of mother,
galloping, with nothing to stop me.

Now in the evening I put on my dress
like a secret; will you see
how my elbow pokes like a hock,
the way I have carefully cut my mane,
the way my eyes roll from fear of you?
I'm trying to hide the animal I am;

and you give me a necklace,
bright as a bit, and you're
stamping your name
into the earth, and my arm
is around you, weak as a halter,
and nothing can stop me, no mother or father.

## A Lunch Date with My Father

As you're speaking I'm dreaming
of leaning over the pizza
of leaning over the salad
of leaning over to stop with a kiss
the sun crashing through the window
like a lion with huge paws.
My father's eyes are black as a canopy,
my father's lip is hard as a tusk,
my father's heart is a broken river;
*beside my father I feel like a vulture.*
Later we embrace like cubs,
whose parents are gone, lost in the sun.

## Take-off

We are rocketing through layers of feeling
to a place that does not feel;
at 10,000 feet I watch the clouds restlessly
impress their frail dreams upon one another;
and though I think of you, you are no more real
than these mouths roaring and dissolving beneath me.
I grow emptier but the plane powers on;
I am leaving everything, leaving you,
like a hat suddenly spiralling up,
to where strangers kiss and death is gone,
and streamers soar in white and blue.

## My Mother Marries My Father

Stitching her neat white wedding hem
I say, *this is how it happens,*
*people pull hardest where there is least love.*
My mother looks at me through violet eyes,
*you don't understand anything.*

Years later I trawl my father
from the ocean of the past
and ask him, did you love her?
His answer is to kiss me on the lips,
his answer is to say, *I've nothing to hide,*
his answer is to watch me
like a fisherman watches a fish out of water,
mourning something, behind blank eyes.

# When I Close My Eyes

When I close my eyes,
the rain pours, like
rain on a foreign window.

Your body is soft
and awkward, as if grief
is finally over.

I hold you like
a survivor, I hold your flesh
like warm sand.

When I close my eyes
the words pour like rain
pouring for the first time.

## Flowers

I hold them like the wrist
of a troublesome child,
I drop them in a bag.
Still trying to touch me, they say
*we are like the foreign country*
*you left but still carry*
*in a book of photographs.*
They think I'm sentimental,
that the dreams I had mean something to me,
that one day I won't be able to do this.

A man cut from the future
is waiting for me in the rain.
The walls are undressed
and left like a child,
the past is tucked for transit
in its familiar box. Later I ask him,
*Did you know I would find you?*
*Am I no longer alone?*
He kisses me among the selves
that never made it this far.

## Excitement

The day has blinked, the streets are awash with blue
the mood of God is lonely;
all day he sent his frozen grief away, unfettered
it swirled and tumbled, unaware of falling.
All day I've waited on the inside,
watching the light grow fat and fade away.
God doesn't know of my excitement,
*look my hands are neatly folded.*
God doesn't know I've been possessed,
*look I'm bright and smartly dressed.*
But my heart's a lump of you,
I'm an empty bed at empty noon;
I'm a stone wall smacked with sunlight,
I'm a stick of rock with KISS stamped through.

## New Forest Ponies

Here come the ponies
down the gutted track,
with old women's chins,
biting for apples, scalloping
the earth with their beggars' legs.
I call to them, my hands
dark as soft apples.

Their warmth is sharper than fire,
their smell licks round me,
hooves crack like twigs;

you're in the car, uneasy
as the ponies clatter noiselessly.
They're coming at me, with their
anger all messy in their hearts.
They're circling me softly
like a body dragged from leaves,
my discarded, hungry dreams
come to find me.

## Walk in the Rain

You walk for miles beside me
through trees that open out too quickly
onto rain-soaked common land.
I tell you almost everything,
I feel it coming out of me, like a sickness.
And you sit beside me
on a bench sodden with rain and the smell of things over
and you're telling me all those things are over,
and you're kissing me because they're all over,
and our bodies drift like leaves on the water,
and the people in the distance are made of water,
and the lake is swallowing, with a million mouths a second,
all the things I ever wanted, all the things that are over.

## Sunset

I watched the sun roll
down the nape of the hill
like a great ball caught by Atlas.

I watched the most perfect gold coin
fall from a careless palm
into nothingness, and all the people

seemed to be standing in rags
at the edge of a biblical flood.
But to the girls on bikes

dodging the rocks in the path and laughing,
to the beautiful girl with
sandstone lips and a terrier called Max,

to the couples with their children,
the dropping of the sun
like the corner of space melting

was nothing to be remarked on;
no more than if you
had looked up from among the swans,

and when I did not move
had crossed the bridge towards me.
Mothers running to their daughters

are a commonplace, and the sun of
unimaginable red, rolling away
and turning the water to death

and the grass to flesh,
leaving the world with no promises,
is a commonplace.

# Amsterdam

Here in Amsterdam the homes
dam the flooding sky
with open sleepy eyes, dreaming
of ordinary things.

My hand in yours in the black and green
of a searing winter;
on the cobbles bikes bounce,
faces stare steadfastly ahead.

We sip tiny beers, we talk of gaps in love;
*please don't say it's us*. Above
the glowing streets, we make love
to foreign sounds, familiar touches;

and later in a blue corner
of the Bourbon, a man
as tall as my father,
with hair twice as white

is speaking inflected English.
He has the stoop of someone
plucked out of love; he has
hands that let his children fall;

and in the heart of Amsterdam
a woman's mouth is open,
and a man is forgetting who she is,
I can feel him forgetting her

in the floor sobbing the blues,
in the jumbled bodies hammering
their weakness, their fury,
into all hope, into a spine of stairs.

# Szechèny Tér

## 1 *The Consultant*

The consultant was draped in white
as if to protect himself from dust
in a great abandoned house.
To the round-faced Hungarian woman he spoke,
who spoke in French to my French friend,
who translated brokenly to me.
In a small polite line we stood
beneath this mountainous man
whose face I dared not look into.
*Tell him*, I hissed up the line, *tell him
if he doesn't do it, I'll do it myself.*
It was as if I'd been left on a frozen hillside
and having unexpectedly survived
was then brought in to meet my maker.
I was trembling so hard I could hardly speak,
my lips were heavy and blue,
conversation screamed around me,
drenching me as though in snow.
*What is he saying?* I whispered, but no one answered.
The consultant had a chest so deep and wide
I might have clambered up on it to die.
It seemed as good a place as any, a place
as indifferent and clean as any.
Then they were filing me out,
someone mad, held together
just by women's hands.
*What is he saying?* I said,
or maybe I said nothing
as they led me away.

II *The Angels*

We were robed in white like angels.
We were taken downwards.
The others would not look at me.

They muttered their spiky language.
Their mothers in their reds and browns
huddled to them like huge birds,

their eyes hard and pale
like beautiful foreign pebbles,
or the painted eyes of the chapel's Mary.

When the doors opened,
nurses like mountain faces
came to take us.

They washed us,
they dressed us,
they stood us in line.

A silent chorus of white
to be wheeled
one by one

into quiet arms
that drained the light from the room
and the fear from us,

sending us out flat as paper,
slack-mouthed and open-wristed,
white robe in disarray,

and rows of angels lifting their heads,
observing without pity
this new bloom of ugly red.

III *The Wish*

I never thought it would hurt me,
but as it found a place
to cling to inside me,
like an almost invisible tern
latching itself to the cliffside,
and all you see is the flash
of unnatural blue when the storm
changes its direction –
as it found somewhere,
it dug in and I cried out.
I knew then. I knew before
I began to lie awake all night
and cook up pasta at 3 a.m.,
before your postcard arrived
coffee-splashed and bright from Idaho,
before the summer burned
itself out, became a shell
through which the winter tore.
It grew colder and colder,
my breasts began to weep.
Stepping out onto the ice, I whispered
*I wish I wish I wish*
but there was no sound from anywhere.
The ice was thick as oil.
I let myself slide
down the corkscrew road,
down, into a strange drowning,
and in its reflection I saw what was inside me,
pale-faced, small, with no comprehensible wish.

## IV  *The Dream*

I can't find the hospital
and each morning that I can't find the hospital,
the old woman stands in the February glare
of Szechèny Tér and holds out
a bunch of snowdrops, doubling
its price just for me.

## Szalon Sör

At first we devoured it,
at 30p, so astoundingly cheap,
dark brown and sweet,
its smell whorling into the air from the sör gyár.
Americans wouldn't touch it,
so goddamn *thick* they complained,
while the locals leant round bottles of it,
their child-tummied bodies
packing the tiny söröző,
their hard laughter
clattering out into the dusty street.

Years on, we've come back
to find most things more faded still,
except the labels on the Szalon
which now show a king with his glass raised,
and horsemen galloping in to crush the Turks,
and with glasses to match,
embossed in brilliant red and gold.
We are thrilled, we barter excitedly
and take a set from the waiter for 500 forints.
We give them pride of place in our living-rooms,
stack our best pens in them.

# How to Love You

With my body?
You can pick that up anywhere:
the top shelf of the newsagent's,
or teasingly obscured in brown paper
where we stop for sweets.
There's nothing special about its
hotchpotch of dark and light,
named, scored, hotly debated.
A long time ago, this hand-me-down body
scored an almost perfect 9.9,
when winter's ice had given me an edge
and the world fell away for an instant,
and I was nothing, and he was nothing too,
and the world was a place where bodies were new as snow.
But that's the kind of thing I'd make up,
the kind of dream I'd embellish for a touch
from a world warmly dressed,
strangely kind to my nakedness;
and so, I don't know how to love you.
With my heart? I believe you know
the heart's full of unknowable blood.
It's no place for you.

# Stephen Selects the Photographs

Stephen's hands are the washed out
magnolia of an old rented room,
his eyes are bleached from years
of striplight through film;

through his soft shirt, slightly open,
his body is thin like a girl-model's,
his shoulders jut as he leans
forensically

into an ordered world of technical detail.
Is it *nice*? Is it *pink*? Is it *neat*?
Somewhere, even far away, is she *smiling*?
It is long ago, I am numbed to the wonder

that a body so slight, so
appealingly slight, can observe another so,
and feel no kinship, no pity,
no welling of tears, nor surprise that it is so.

These are strange facts to possess:
how a naked body lies
as if sorry in the hands,
how flesh breaks namelessly open. Facts like this

aren't mine. Mine are the lowered eyes
as wearily you squint through slide after slide,
a quietly disgusted Aryan soldier
whose fingertip indicates this way or that.

I found you kind back then,
I thought my prayers were love-songs
muttered in the street
and in the arms of men:

may you always find me *nice*
let me be not *slag* or *dog*
may I never make you angry
may you never turn on me.

## Letter to the Man I Love

When feeling cheated, remember
that you are loved
by the only one who didn't cry.
This may seem small consolation,
and perhaps you would prefer
that you were not loved by
someone of such monumental achievement.
Please, let me explain.
I have watched as people are stripped naked
and invited to writhe on the floor.
I do not know them, nor
what they may have done to deserve this.
I have, however, invented names for them, and stories
about how much they enjoy it.
I have filled their mouths with lies,
and I have answered letters from the general public
as if I were them, repeating those lies.
I have written their confessions
which were totally untrue
and received payment for the forgery.
I have given, on request,
photos of them in various poses to friends
and even to my own father (who was delighted)
in order to make myself more popular (which it did).
I have, on social occasions, announced
that my varied tasks I find 'liberating',
and on that basis have found myself,
on more than one occasion
embodying those lies.
I have answered phone calls from the general public
who wish to know in *exactly* what way
I would like to be stripped
and pushed to the floor,

with scrupulous politeness,
following the company code that all callers are customers.
I have not, until now,
questioned out loud
the glaring fact that all these people
stripped and lied about
are not unlike myself, and that I
have written about them as if they were dogs or mice
because that is the only way to lie about them convincingly.
Nor have I, until today,
when I couldn't stop crying,
realised the impossibility of love
with someone to whom
I have lied so much.

## Casualty Report

As though I would survive,
I forgave the digging of my body
in preparation for war.
I had my basic training,

I clutched my rations to me
and counted them at night.
At dawn I pushed aside the corpses
and went over the top.

I stumbled through no man's land,
living miracle after miracle,
that I could still hurt, that I still lived,
that I might reach the other side.

They gave me a badge and an office
and I ignored the devastation,
the bodies upright as though neatly shot,
the corpses guzzling in their suits,

the long corridors all leading to loss,
the empty screens crackling against my fingers.
As though I would survive
I *became good*, I *learned to love*.

At night I curled and dreamed
I was alive. By day I neatly filed
my names away, ticking as appropriate
squandered, stolen, marched away at gunpoint.

## Crime of Passion

The cow is the good woman,
the woman we'd like to be.
The cow dips her blunt lips
into the slow river.
She's sleek, she eats well;
her udder, heart of her cowishness,
sways like a pleasant mushroom she's quietly cultivating.
The cow is never angry.
She wears her yellow tag indifferently,
like an heirloom she's too young to know the meaning of.
The cow hasn't got a nasty bone in her body,
from fat brown eye to foot split in two
she's a slurping awkward dome of contentment
who doesn't understand
and forgets soon after
the hot afternoon
when a woman brought them biscuits

and the cows shambled mildly into a circle,
bubbles of snot cracking from their friendly noses,
their tongues like slabs of live pink custard
investigating their nostrils, as they edged
closer and closer without interest or meaning,
blowing their grassy breath into her face,
their tails swishing away the light,
the panicky flies, the air
growing hotter and darker;
shambling off a short time later
over a strange crushed earth, wetter than flesh.

## My Education at the Zoo

There is a rule which I am born knowing,
from the moment I slip out, and my mouth

becomes that anguished, red, newborn hole,
its ridge of unborn teeth uselessly bared.

I know this rule and am flailing against it.
But in later years I come to an uneasy acceptance;

my unusual physical strength is a testament
to its weight. When I am sixteen

I can push a barrow overflowing
with rolling cow haunch and pony carcass

all the way up the hill to the wolves.
Only the strongest of the strong men can do it:

there is laughter, and something else, a recognition.
On New Year's Eve, when one year metamorphoses

into a dream of another, they kiss me
with uneasy, snarling kisses.

The Amazon parrot whirls at me,
a green screech as I approach his nest;

next door, the cockatoo is pacing up and down,
he clambers up me, as if I were a gnarled tropical tree,

lodges his head down my shirt between my breasts,
murmurs (you must incline your head to hear his words)

*fuck you bitch*, his yellow eyes blinking.
I'm afraid at the end I begin to fall apart,

and accidentally set three pairs of lovebirds free
and the cockatoo, who simply climbs the nearest tree

and hurls insults (but suddenly the words begin to come,
secretly, when I am alone at night).

The real men bask at lunchtime, like lions keeping
their violence to themselves while the sun is hot.

At night, at party after party, I find it hard
to keep from being discovered or blurting the truth.

I drink ten pints, laugh at all insults,
refuse to retreat, as finally amidst howls

of laughter at 3 a.m., one of them emerges
wearing two bras and a nightie, his face covered in paint,

and everyone cheering his victory in the game
that he is playing, that now I know the name of.

# Dora

> In 1900 Sigmund Freud treated 'Dora', a girl of 18, for what was at that time termed hysteria. His analysis concluded that it was her repressed desires that had caused her symptoms. Dora disagreed and terminated treatment.

There's a lot wrong with me.
Saying it makes me ugly.
I don't know how to say it, I
don't know how to say
what has happened to me.

Alone, I try not to remember.
The truth has shaped itself into a parody of me,
curled up in me like a baby,
a sinful ugly baby
that cannot be loved, nor delivered.

The truth has no words.
Without words there can be no "facts".
And Dr Freud wants facts from me.
*Tell me what happened*, he says. I offer him
my stumbling, manacled dreams.

He says I'm in love with Herr K.
He says I'm in love with Frau K.
He says I'm in love with my father.
He says I'm probably in love with him.
Can't he see what happens

when words confront the truth?
They scatter like rats.
They become non-words, non-sense.
I am dulled, as if a long stoning
finally is ending.

If I yield, he promises
*there will be comfort.*
I would like to be comforted.
Sir, we will do without comfort
we will do without it –

excuse my breathlessness as I stand,
my unsteadiness, my ugly limp.
My body still tries, you see,
to say it, to push it out of me,
what happened to me.

# Baby

How many of us begin this way –
a scheme by one or other, a plot
to manufacture love, dreamt up
by tellers weary of their story.

Always I believed that to exist
one must be loved. Now I dream
a more wearied story, whose plot
shows the stuff I'm made of.

The baby downstairs cries. Is she
loved enough to sway the story?
She knows neither weariness nor dreams,
nor that this particular plot

was written long before she came.
She is their story's epitaph,
the end of love, its weary dream:
a plot of earth, well tended.

# The Pet Rabbit

I can't call it love, I call it *white*,
a slash of rock, a touchable sky,
colourless, but swallowing light
with hollowed out hands and misshapen eye,
stooping to smell me and whispering *my*
as it scoops me up from the muddied rain,
mumbling dumbly, an attempt to explain

its need of me, its fear of being alone,
for which I am the talisman, a familiar black,
set in a box like a glittering stone
where it nourishes me as though I were its lack,
bringing fragments of life, holding a universe back,
and at the end of the day taking sound and all light
to an easier sleep, to a dream-filled night.

## The Walk of Faith

can stand the weight of five baby elephants.
I cannot do it, I cannot cross a square of glass
though you hold my hand though you
point out that I weigh less than five baby elephants.
It is not the fear of falling,
but the fear of disobedience –
of walking where I was not meant to walk,
of seeing people tiny, vulnerable,
without civilisation or meaning.
I have no faith: I could not cross and be unchanged.
The source of my giddiness: I am a speck in the sky
and *no one remembers me*. And at the same time
I know the tiny scattered creatures
whom we observe with mild loathing
and some pity are me. They are all me,
running without direction, as if I had plummeted though
the five-baby-elephant-proof glass and had
shattered on North Shore and all the pieces
had picked themselves up and were scuttling away.
Look – that one crosses the road a little too recklessly,
is narrowly missed by a tram, is tearing away from something.
There – another has flung her arms around a man in the street,
a man whom she thought was her father,
and indeed he seems not unwilling to take on the role,
he has embraced her, he is kissing her hair,
telling her *I will try anything twice* and laughing.
But look there: a crowd has gathered,
a circle around somebody dead in the road,
it's someone whose hate has got the better of them,
someone who's gone and got themselves killed,
and somebody's sister is sprinting towards the Pleasure Beach
– I can see from here that she's not going to make it –

the crowds are gaining on her, the swoop of the big dipper
is impossibly far away –
that other place, where people fall and do not break,
I cannot reach it, no faith I know of
can get me there.

# Dear Virginia Ironside

I thought my wife and I
enjoyed an excellent sex life,
but recently she informed me
that on the point of orgasm
she feels like smashing up the room
and stamping on the pieces,
she imagines breaking my teeth
and slashing the walls with broken glass,
she feels like a shark in a feeding frenzy,
as if she's drenched in blood
and no one knows her any more.
It puts her off, she says.
We used to make love all the time,
but now she says she's afraid of something.
She lies awake all night.
Sometimes she even cries.
I want to comfort her.
I almost reach out.
But I'm afraid that if I do
something else will come out,
a deeper fury, even worse,
and I won't know who it belongs to.

# The Writing on the Fridge

We unsnap the pieces
of our new-bought Erotic Poetry
and gigglingly announce
our *glistening apparatus*,
our *pubic joy*, our
*languid moaning nipples*.
But soon we're out of prepositions,
pronouns (special pack required),
something to let us know
who's doing what to whom.
Our fridge is swaggering
but ultimately inarticulate.
*Show me what you want*, he says,
and through the hungry words I search,
like a child scanning half-familiar crowds
pouring from an unknown place.
He's watching me eagerly
as I take out the scissors
and *snip! snip! snip!*
turn a handful of words into babble.
Through the corner of my eye
I watch his smile,
observe how it freezes,
as an unbelievable story spells itself out
one letter at a time,
uneven and frantic.

## Bears

About a week afterwards,
she sees the first one,
curled between the cornflakes and the ketchup.
Its eyes are tight shut, two thin lines,
its long eyelashes quivering
with each invisible breath.
It's small enough to fill two palms,
and when she checks again
it's sleeping still,
as if only the lightest breath
could wake it.

Next day, she almost hot-washes one.
There it was, alone in the drum
like a child's mitten.
Her husband says nothing.
His mouth keeps the truth tightly in.
That night she wakes to find him sleeping
with two bears curled on his chest.

Now there are nearly twenty.
She took to feeding them at midnight
and suddenly they multiplied.
A saucer of milk on the kitchen floor,
and plump shadows come to life,
tiny lumberings across the lino,
to slurp in a circle like hedgehogs.
When she curls beside them
they rest their round snouts
on every tired crook of her.

She takes to sleeping on the floor,
clinging to the warmth of them,
even when blood seeps
from the ear of the smallest,
and they start to snarl over the milk
and in her dreams all day and night
their cries come, high pitched and thin.

# Pilate Comes to My Father's Deathbed

On the last day
they summoned me, and I came to his bedside.
When I asked him, *so, you are the king?*
he merely smiled. I looked to his followers.
One said, *I do not care what he has done*
and the others said nothing.

It was a difficult case.
He did not express remorse, nor love.
His only word was *discomfort*
as the nurses turned him a last time.

I looked for a sign
that there was a case to answer. It seemed
that there was, and there was not.
I heard of no tenderness, nor compassion.
But there was a framed photo
and a daughter, and a son.

I said to them, *shall I stop this?*
and they merely wept.
I said to him, *do you understand my authority?*
*Speak. Justify yourself.*

He said nothing
and I was decided.
When the others could not bear
to see the drop of his head,
the sweating of his skin,
the blindness of his eyes,
I took my place by his face.

And when his gasps drew no air
and his frantic heart jumped
and his hand grew icy
I did nothing.
I could see no case to answer.
I turned him over to his own people.

**Progress Diary**

I've tried everything else; I'll try this.
*Forget yourself.* It's a glossy idea. Costs a packet.
Day one: everyone's crying without actually crying.
Everyone's loveless, penniless, hopeless,
and hungry, hungry, hungry.
Comfort 2 people. Shed 0 tears.

Day two: my father's dying, disastrously slowly.
I touch the hands of people I've never met.
They've come to cry and end up crying.
*Loss can be assuaged by others.*
But they say my hands are cold.
Comfort 3.5 people. Shed 0 tears.

Day three: I've salvaged a pen and a camera.
I take pictures, but the cold is terrible.
There's a fog I can't see through. I talk
to anyone who'll listen, even though it's against the rules.
They turn their heads ever-so-slightly.
But I've thrown open the door and I can't stop.
The weak light bathes me in stillness.
I stuff the air with words.
I can't stop until I retch.
Comfort 0 people. Shed (approx) 3 tears.

Day five: Last night I remembered him. I heard the room say
*forever*. I am fuzzy headed, cold.
Comfort 0 people. Shed 0 tears.

# Metamorphosis

> It happens that I'm tired of being a man.
> PABLO NERUDA, 'Walking Around'

It happens that in the morning
just before I wake, when the world
lays its palms gently upon my eyes,
it happens that my cheekbones are hollow,
and a damp pallor inhabits my skin.
The final ugliness of death,
like that of the sick predator
with slow blinking eyes, I feel it enter me.
Father, I've been writing to you.
I've been touching your picture.
I've been drafting and redrafting
your certainty that it wasn't over.
You wrote on a corner of paper
*don't panic*. Father, it happens
that your tired skin has been delivered to me.
Someone's gathered it up in the dawn air.
Someone's wrapping it round me.
My mouth's open in a death yawn,
my fingers are heavy,
my legs thin and untouchable.
I'm struggling to wake, but it seems so far away.
I feel a flutter of pain through fog,
I turn myself with difficulty.
Father, it happens that I die like this
each dawn, each half-sleep.
Later, when I am dressed, and for all the world
a woman, I catch sight of myself in the mirror.
Death has left a trace of its ugliness.
You've etched it into me, my heritage.
Father, it happens that I'm tired with the weight of it,
the knife of your face, the stones of your hands.

# Kleptomaniac

There are things which you gave me:
a bundle of letters written in green,
a man's nose, a curly way of writing 'P';
and there are things which I *took*:
this unsmiling photograph,
this t-shirt, the taste of you washed out of it.

In a bright hospital
you offered your death to me.
You gave it slowly over months
then crazily, hand over fist.
You let me come when others must not come.
You let me sit beside you through the night.
This is vulnerability, the gift tag said,
your gift to me.

But of course it wasn't enough.
I couldn't stop a habit so long engrained.

On the last night, I snatched
a long look at you when we were alone.
I half-inched
a touch from your hand on my mouth
that you would never have allowed.
I lifted
your smile at the sound of my name
and I ran with it.

Like a stolen child
that all of Scotland Yard
and all the world's fathers are searching for,
I shut it in a dark place
where I wrapped it
over and over
in my delight.

# My Faithless Mouth

It was my mouth
suddenly on the bus,
my faithless mouth
which I had sworn to silence.
My mouth, the filthy whorish thing
threw itself open on the bus
in front of all the schoolboys
and the mums on their way to the Co-op.
No sound came out,
but that was of no consequence:
the secret was out
and all the scraps of hospital
that I'd been trying to hold onto
began to worm their way out of my eyes.
My mouth, shocked at what it had begun,
tried to close itself.
It turned my head to the window
so that only the lonely wife
dusting the butterflies
nailed to the outside of her home
looked and looked away.
I coughed. I waved. I pulled out a magazine.
My mouth, in the glare of publicity,
forgot everything and slipped offstage.
I grabbed my eyes and cheeks and nose
which now were sliding down my neck
and stuffed them in my bag,
striding blankly from the bus.
I ran whimpering home.
We sat on the edge of the bed.
I could see that he was terrified.
He said, 'Don't worry. It's all right.'
as from the hole where my mouth had been
popped a plump leg, an oil slick wing.

FROM
# Take Me with You
(2005)

## The Poetry God

has golden hair,
wears a golden ring.

He carries a red valise
in which two pairs of shoes

walk the inner edge.
He likes *things*.

The Poetry God says
*Do you want to be here or not?*

*If you fear you are alone
a poem is a kind of love.*

We lie down together
in a faded room.

We get on with the business
of filling the empty page.

## My Life, the Sea

There was a time when I was empty
and my life was ravenous: it lapped at me
though I had nothing to give it.
It yowled in the rolling rooms I inhabited,
it pawed the lovers who followed me there
to see what they were made of, recoiling
when it found them full of gold and blood.
I was weak and I lied to my life.
It sobbed at the shore as I left, its face ugly,
its breath sour. It swore to drink itself to death.
I opened my mouth to the sky and the sun.
I was free as a ghost. I stopped speaking.
I hid myself in crowds and a new language.
Sometimes phones would ring when I passed them.
Sometimes letters would reach me, torn into pieces.
I never spoke of my life and it did not find me,
except at night when I rolled wide awake
and it slept in my arms like a beautiful fish.

## The Voyage of the Rays

Skirts fluttering,
they melt through the water,
rippling the sleep of the boat.

Each gasps a satisfaction
at the haul from sea into fire,
the flash of hands,

the scorch of the floor.
Each beats her tail feebly, rolls the sun
over the gloss of her spine,

her bleeding lip pressed
against a window of wood.
Her message is her body

winded at his feet,
eyes sinking in relief
at the journey completed.

He throws each back,
watches her turn, a medal in space,
but still they keep coming,

surfacing like dreams he has no answer to,
filling all the ocean
with trembling politeness.

## Swan

I thought that it was you
turning to me for an instant
from the blindness of the water,

a pure white question,
with its underwater dream in tow
softening the stones at my feet.

I thought that it was you
and if not you, then love itself
tacking perfectly towards me,

rocking in its own beauty,
the circles backing out
like people not quite believing.

# Fishing Boat

I wanted so much to save it,
the carved sea, the white sky
bleaching me away.

The peregrines whipped from the chalk,
rushed up the cliff-face
like ash from the baking sea,

and I wanted so much to save it,
how we lay down, and the sun
fired our shadows into the rock.

Far below a fishing boat chugged
like a toy, pushing its blue V
to somewhere familiar,

and I saw the skipper recording,
I saw that he would be the one
to draft the flutter of clothes,

the obliteration of skin by sun,
the *are they...? are they...?*
as the boat led him out of sight

of the dust and pebbles kicked
slowly down the chalky face.
I saw him scribbling the whispers,

the madness, the too-little time,
as the boat and its trawl of glimpses
slipped away from me, towards home.

## Hedgehog

Its leg was not broken. It was not homeless.
It clenched in my hands, a living flinch.
*You cannot love so much and live,*
it whispered, its spines clicking like teeth.
I hid it from itself in a cardboard box.

Overnight it nibbled a hole and slipped away.
I cried so much my mother thought I'd never stop.
She said, *you cannot love so* – and yet
I grew to average size and amused a lot of people
with my prickliness and brilliant escapes.

## Elvis the Performing Octopus

hangs in the tank like a ruined balloon,
an eight-armed suit sucked empty,

ushering the briefest whisper
across the surface, keeping

his slurred drift steady with an effort
massive as the ocean resisting the moon.

When the last technician,
whistling his own colourless tune,

splashes through the disinfectant tray,
one might see, had anyone been left to look,

Elvis changing from spilt milk to tumbling blue,
pulsing with colour like a forest in sunlight.

Elvis does the full range, even the spinning top
that never quite worked out, as the striplight fizzes

and the flylamp cracks like a firework.
Elvis has the water applauding,

and the brooms, the draped cloths, the dripping tap,
might say that a story that ends in the wrong place

always ends like this –
fabulous in an empty room,

unravelled by the tender men in white,
laid out softly in the morning.

# Nibbling

Devastated cobwebs
cling to her lashes. She's

a crazed dictator, disappearing
whole families of scorching pink.

The pin faces of forget-me-nots
giggle as she opens wide.

She rips the hearts out of dandelions
and snaps the backs of mint in two.

In dreams I take her with me,
tightly in my arms,

and I set her gently down
wherever lawns have lost their mind.

## Buffalo Mozzarella

When I say that I tasted him
I mean that I knew the stale
baby-press of his mouth,
his cold breath, and the way
he scratched the cushion of his thumb
on his stubbled cheek. See –

how he leans in the litter bin,
his arm digging deep,
to feel among the cut of beer cans
the abominable plastic, the rub of old fat,
as if there should be flesh there,
something gentle to welcome him.

And then he finds it – the sundried tomato
and buffalo mozzarella sandwich
I had just one bite out of because I saw
the one thing that scared me most,
and I dropped my sandwich with its one
shell-shaped ticklishly damp bite out.

I didn't think that a mouth
more silent than mine
would nuzzle where my lips had been
and bite out a shape to caress mine,
nibbling, delicate, not rushing at all –
and that someone else's hunger

and sorrow and spit would devour mine.
When I say that I tasted him
I mean that the night shook me awake
and I saw the back of his head clearly
as he bent down into darkness and shame
to find out the truth about me.

# Baize

I should have tried harder
to love Steve Davis.
If not for his neat bow tie
then for his rare motor skills.

Good hand-eye co-ordination
smooths the path of a relationship.
At least one of you must have it,
like hope, and the ability

to love and keep one's word.
There was much I failed to understand
that Steve tried to explain:
that life's a process of elimination,

and the black truth must be toyed with
until it's the only way out.
One must maximise one's options
within the frame the game creates,

avoiding conflict until its result
can be decisive in your favour –
and the one true art is procrastination
so complex it appears something is happening

until finally, the smack of the cue
drives uncertainty off the face of the earth.
I've learned at last I don't need anything
that requires a hand to touch me.

I dream of the long green baize
where Steve and I might have lain,
my unmanageable dreams
finally, gratefully, pocketed.

# The Lexicographer Finishes P

There's going to be a party when they finish P,
he says. He's only a part-time lexicographer,
at heart he is a poet. I sip
and wonder how he can resist escape
from the palace which is really a prison
into the secret tunnel of O or the labyrinth of Q.
He's a palimpsest: in his hands are the shadows
of F and faint etching of K, and one deep swirl of C.
With such ease he's abandoned one letter for another,
in love with the primitive after enjoying the modern,
a pantheist who no longer answers to God.
I want to tell him,
*take me with you.*
I'm passionate enough for P,
I get palpitations when I think of perfection;
I believe in paradise, I believe in the permanent,
(and in possibilities), today I'm a pasque-flower,
tomorrow a paramour. I can learn to keep my peace.
There is a pause.
He's perturbed, pouting, pushing away his cappuccino.
*I've even changed my name*, I say. *Please.*

## Nagyvázsony Castle
*Balaton, Hungary*

There was a time when I was buried
deep in the walls of a far ruin

and it was not language that saved me,
nor was it history, nor was it me at all,

but the way that certain people can sense
warmth through stone and start pulling.

Far below, my friends are laughing,
children squeal to the stocks and the dungeon.

The green country I remember reaches out,
sunflowers break its heart, vines stitch it whole.

I remember the incantation,
the laying on of hands,

my blanket as I got to my feet,
the command to be forever amazed.

# Proposal from the Bottle Bank

I am taking the empties to the bottle bank.
The car clinks like a nervous ice cream van.
When I open the boot, the green wine-eyes wink.

I lay the crates in the mud of footprints.
My face is wet. When I lick my fingers I taste you.
I sweat like the hot hours before a hangover.

The first bottle breaks and I imagine your dress
around your waist, your face turned away.
You are cool against me. You are *softness*.

The hole of the bank is rusted and hungry.
Like your mouth it takes whatever I give it.
The smell of wine, sharp as grief, swallows me.

They fall one by one into the dark.
*Will you love this? Forever?* I ask,
in the swirling rain, multicoloured as trash.

# My Husband

lives by the sea.
His windows shudder in sea storms.
The gun-blue clouds drift

across the waves like airships.
My husband has a red wine stain
across his expensive white carpet.

I knocked over my glass
the first time I went there.
I didn't mention the husband-thing.

I think of my husband
as the city whispers
like a hungry, birdless ocean.

I keep the phone close
in case he should decide
to come and save his wife.

# Dumbarton

In changing my life I got as far as Dumbarton.
It was midnight. She didn't believe I loved her,
so I rang her and said, *I'm getting in the car now*
and I found myself swallowing the road out of Glasgow,
the bridge screaming at me to leave then, leave.

I rang her. I hated my voice. *I'm so tired
darling, tired*, I said. The click told me
that the future is as uncertain as the past.
The road was empty, my whole body ached.
I had nine points on my licence and so

had to crawl my way to my brand new life.
She didn't believe I loved her. I rang her.
*I've left everything for you*, I said. Or,
*You're everything to me*. Or perhaps
I said nothing at all, being smashed

upside-down in the central reservation.
The lights of Dumbarton were mostly out
as I turned back. The stars were gibberish,
the road flat on its back. I rang her. I hated my voice.
*I'm so tired, darling, tired. Forgive me.*

## Your Wife

I think of your wife.
She is real and warm
as a cat in my arms.

She smiles at the top of a staircase.
She dreams like a cat,
a murmur that wakes no one.

When I think of your wife
you are leaving her.
She glances up at the first word.

And afterwards
someone leads her
to the edge of a bright ocean.

She cannot escape it
though she writes herself a raft
and clambers on it.

I send her a message in a bottle.
She lifts her head in the sun.
Will she open it?

Her hair is plastered to her face.
But she knows you.
She unwraps my message,

finds a poem that she scans
a thousand times.
I think of your wife

as you lay me
beneath you
and what I feel

when your hands are on me
is no pain
and white peace

like a sky filling everything.
I think of nothing.
Nothing I want is shocking.

# Mule

He snaps five halters before I learn
that four hooves dug in means no.
I try weeping. I try weaving

a trail of Polos down the yard.
I tickle him under the chin.
He regards me without amusement.

I think he loves me, even as he sinks
his long teeth into my head when I drag
his foreleg an inch. I cry at his feet.

I nibble hay and try to understand.
I gather the Polos and feed them to him.
His lips are wet and grateful.

This is the language of refusal,
the eternal tenderness
of things that will not move.

By sunrise, he is my creature
and this is my home.
I cry and I beat him. I do not leave.

## Women

I sail into the world of women,
in a magnificent ship that does not interest them.

I imagine this is what loving them is:
adding up the piecework of them,

the pale neck, the sudden crow's feet,
the expensive lips saying *of course of course.*

I have learned their language, I can say
*what do you think?* like a native,

but they detect an accent in spite of me.
Their eyes rest on me over the wine.

Their secrets are palpable as money.
We trade, and I grow rich. I feel free.

We compare songs, the cuts on our wrists.
Sometimes I think I have found my home.

When I hold them, I hear their bones crying.
Their costly hair drifts and shines.

# Two Views of Loch Long

I *Dance*

In the evening when the loch
ruffles like a skirt made of steel
my father comes back from the dead
to show me his latest steps.

He loved to dance; he danced until
he could no longer hold the women to him,
until he fell down in the street, got back up,
each step an awkward new-learned move.

But not tonight. Tonight he holds me
and I feel his warmth against my face.
He says (everything the dead say is new)
*Close your eyes. Remember me.*

I go back into the kitchen, say hello
to someone, put on the radio.
His warmth haunts my hands for hours.
I touch a cup. The world moves.

II **Lost Property**

I search my thoughts of you.
I want to say, *Here is the reason*

*you should be with me*. I have found it.
I keep everything, from kissed matchboxes

to guides to Shanklin Chine.
That poet's sweater for example:

I made him give it to me and I wore it everywhere
though people laughed at the way it dwarfed me.

This item will explain it all.
We made it. It is smooth and deep.

We made it, together in the dark
like a careful surgeon and a clever tailor

who discover one night they are one and the same.
I have searched for days. I have not slept.

I would know it anywhere.
Its moon is missing.

Do you remember? At night
its waters fill with moving light,

like the first wheel ever made
each spoke perfect and on fire.

## Two Views of a Submarine
*Loch Long*

   **I**

The loch is a factory where darkness
is welded and sparked into life,

sent up to breathe like a whale,
the water shattering from its back.

Ferries cross in shiny home-comings,
the loch trembles with a soft pulse

and an echo is sent to live in my skin.
It is a call to witness a miracle:

my wish in its flat black hat
ballooning out of the waves.

## II

When I imagined exactly this
tilt and drift into the dark

I thought I would go mad for you,
that I would forgive everything.

But as I slowly press these walls
like Alice in her Wonderland

who was a child, and simply
reached for whatever caught her eye

and then suddenly did not fit her life,
I know that I would give you up

instantly for oxygen, or hope.
My murmured bargain creaks:

it is being considered, deeply.
I close my eyes and my wish

is granted: I wake open-mouthed,
drenched, cold, in flickering air.

## Still Life with Table and Loch
*Kilcreggan, Scotland*


The long gleam with dead flowers,
the china bowl of small essentials.

The clutter of objects, domestic or hopeful,
the mug of wine with its grubby sheep,

and at the edge a woman asleep,
a woman who still calls herself a girl,

desperate as she is for submarines to turn
to doves or secret monsters.

The birdbath is empty but eager,
its plain face damp with imaginings,

but the horizon is not sentimental:
once again, it explains the violet islands.

The loch is posing for itself today,
starlet-blue, its mermaid tail out to sea.

Its waters are dimpled and young.
It remembers very little today.

# Wave

A low, restless shore,
and a high sun,
sharp as the blade-red
of the oystercatchers
hustling the old sea.

It was just a walk:
no thought to think through,
no fear to work through,
my shadow inconsequential,
my step too light

to dislodge the periwinkles
sucking hard on the rocks,
a grubby, rough population
with its head down. So why
at every step behind me,

did the rockpools clink
and the shingle tock-tick
as the shells let slip and rolled?
I stopped, checked the sun,
jostled my shadow.

It raised itself, my lazy chill,
and the periwinkles fell
with a blaze of shell-shine
into the wave my dark arm
promised but did not bring.

There was no anger at God
for not delivering the sea.
Just the sighs of the tiny
and upside-down, resigned
to the never-rock, the un-brine.

## Fairytale

I search for our story;
my footprints follow
unthinkingly, an untidy line.

A kingfisher sparks
and flickers ahead of me
and of course I follow it

though it leads me only
to where the ducks in formation
know the secret of what comes next.

They drag their perfect lines
until they make sense,
title them with circles,

and send me a rowing boat
with a cargo of voices
and a splash as sharp as a photograph.

I search for our story
down the darkening path
and all that follows

brings me back to this:
to the water, the bridge
and the impossible task,

and the kingfisher's break
from an opening line
bright like a flash of the last.

## Defenestration

You with that gentle look,
she trusts you, and trust is essential

when you're going in for the push.
Which window should it be?

Top of the Pécs TV Tower?
The Eiffel? You there, at the end –

what are you waving about? Tell her what?
That *nothing changes* if she goes or stays,

but there's a way to stop the pain
and you're a helping hand?

Brilliant! Give that man a drink!
I love the elegance of the agreed demise.

Now you know the drill: a quick press
to the heart and a swift turnaround –

no one likes to be observed
when they're losing their grip.

And choose a cold day, a flooded day,
with no sunlight and no people,

a day when even you'd believe
there's just no point in going on.

## Desiderata

Believe your eyes. When he crumples
it is because a memory has woken

and knocked his legs from under him.
Be always kind: hold out your arms

and find a way not to speak. Silence
is much more valuable than words.

Remember we are all wounded. Try
to see his suffering without panic

that it will crawl from him to you,
and block out all the light in the sky.

It may do this, but it does not mean to.
It is the nature of pain to eat everything.

Forgive all that will be done to you.
Extend your definition to include now.

Believe in everything, time after time.
Dream of caution. Never be yourself.

# Domestic Science

My attempts to boil you
out of him failed:
you rose to the surface

like foam in a whisky vat,
and he gulped you back down
faster than I could scrape you off.

I spent months hoovering
the flakes of you off him.
He didn't thank me for it.

He searched the rubbish
to replace the dust in his hair.
He screamed when I tried

to remove your jagged face
from his chest. He wept.
Our life was a bloody mess:

filleting you out was our only hope.
His pain rang like breaking glass.
My tears made no difference.

He stopped mentioning you at all.
We talked of the place that lies
beyond all this. He cooked supper

and opened a nice bottle of wine
while I laid everything in a circle
to make sure we got there.

# Rainbow

We push a trolley through Kitchens
filled with bright things on which we agree.
We buy candles, a water jug, and (nearly)

a cutlery set. Not a life yet but nearly,
bringing home the giddy truth:
*a new beginning*. We've been so clumsy

but see how the plates shine unbroken?
We shake our heads at Curtains and Lighting
press on through Office Organisation,

just sure enough of what we have
not to ask for too much, yet. We touch down
in Bedrooms, with time arching over us

and our bodies restless. Which frame
will frame us best? Which keep us safe?
Outside the road is pouring with rain,

unbroken for days, but the car starts first time
and we're on our way home, blinking through water,
our treasures clinking in their muddy chest.

## XX

They met in Rome, above the ruins of the Forum. Yours was on her first trip in a brand new life of sobriety, and mine had wandered off from his wife and children, and found himself in a new country. They stood next to each other amazed at the jumble laid out before them, and at exactly the same moment each raised a cigarette to their lips. 'Looks like all my coincidences,' he remarked and she, without turning to look, said, 'It looks like my life,' which was clever, but rather serious, and he thought he might cry. For no reason she could think of, she decided to say you were dead, and strangely she felt free now, was that a terrible thing to say? He said he understood completely, some things only end when a person dies. He almost said, *Do you ever think your life would make more sense without you in it?* but by then it was mid-afternoon and the sun was crawling in the ruins, so they agreed to meet later when the day had cooled to tell each other swashbuckling stories about fate and chance, whose endings you and I dream of, and whose beginnings – in the end – no longer feature us.

## My America

Afterwards, I set sail for you.
I hear that no matter

how I lay myself,
tight and frightened

or clean and full of forgiveness,
there's room to start again.

I know life will be hard,
carved from first principles,

there are enemies to crush
with everything we've got.

There are skies to scrape
and a past to speed from

till it's a tiny grey island
that no one remembers.

I land exhausted, with only
a suitcase, broken open,

and at your feet I begin
my book of declarations

that will be our history,
that will make us brand new people.

## Beijing

At night the city exhales,
a beast of neon and fog.

By day it grows and forgets,
tiny people pick across

its shoulders, nipples and teeth.
Hundreds fall off each day

in an act of cheap forgetting.
We travel the scars of its skin

towards a sky scraped through
to the blue. My eyes a crane,

I lift faces, swing them back
and forth. I feel I know them,

their machine-blankness,
the factory of their speech.

Far above me, builders clink,
sharp against the sun as children.

This is the making, making,
that our bodies are slave to,

forgetful of losses, of blood,
of ancient, useless, waves of love.

# Chengdu Massage

I lie tidy as an English village
while her fingers sting me with sleet,
her snowball fists smash into me.
She pads around me, light as a coot,
before hammering exploding nails
into my thighs – then on to my temples,
pressing till my eyes spark –
and I see nothing but China's
electric bones, its face of fog –
and my own giant muteness, piled and blind,
unlovely and stubborn as cement.

## Flights Over Siberia

And then we tip, with giddy slowness,
like an ice cube or a smooth green olive
drifting through a long, clear gin.
When I see you again we will each have shed
half a world, and ourselves as we go,
as if we were dying forever at high speed.
Below lies the skeletal desert, its spine of ash,
its hide crusted and still, the last thing I see
before I close the blind and turn to sleep.
We each have seen the same forbidden blue,
the same fire too bright to believe, and it is this
that means we hold each other after the fall
of five thousand miles, and know we are alive.

## Bride

A bride is the chosen sort,
in the right place at the right time,
with the right plans in the right order.
Today the book falls open at the right page,
the light, though wrong for winter, is right,
my body and my thoughts feel right:
my head, for once, is screwed on right.
I was a child. I peered at life, in awe
of its wrong heart, its right words, its ruthless correctness.
I shut it out. I longed for it. It embarrassed me.
This is what it is to be a bride:
I leave the shore where I paced my life.
My pleas for the waves to part, or stop,
are swallowed by the gulls who have forgotten me.
There's a raft now, and every time I add a mark
to my strange map, there is a hand on mine.

FROM
# Farewell My Lovely
(2009)

*I Thought It Was in Scotland*

A FALKLANDS WAR STORY

# Landing

Just to make things more frustrating
they show us porno films all night.

Rapiers are breaking up in the hold.
No news in case it puts us off.

In April, it's the height of winter.
When we land the sea is bright blue.

I thought it was in Scotland.
I thought it would be like *Platoon*.

The planes roar in & and drop & turn.
The beach blows up before my eyes

and the thought crosses my mind –
I was going to take Stacey to meet

my parents, but I never did.
And I never slept with her either.

I said goodbye from a phone box.
Couldn't wait for the pips to cut me off.

## Not a Crap Hat

Now maybe I've been tabbing
for fifteen hours or more

and every step is stabbing
and every breath's a chore

and the point of rendezvous
of Operation Lucky Bastard

is in snow that can't been seen through
that's coming fucking faster –

and though these things are true
and I don't want to die here

this is what the Paras do
and I'm on the winning side here

and I wear my red beret
and I wear my Para wings

and you bet that come what may
I'm the master of these things.

---

A 'crap hat' is a derogatory slang term used by paratroopers and commandos to refer to regiments or corps who wear the standard beret.

## May Your God Go with You

It's not what you expect
your sergeant to say

straight after *we expect
to overpower the enemy*

*in two hours or less.*
Eyebrows go up.

What the fuck was that?
He just finished saying

*helicopters are on hand
to airlift the injured.*

*The injured will be back
on ship in twenty minutes.*

We're on the starting line
like the fucking Grand National.

I was all right till he said that.
I was all right till he said that.

## Wild Horses

They were sleeping in their trenches.
I could hear the bastards breathing

but back we crept, to make a plan
(discipline makes the Paras win).

Then we saw them
shifting in the mist.

There was nowhere to escape to
and no time to escape

so we threw ourselves down
and pressed our lips to the mud

and we knew we were dead men
as the hot stench of them

roared over us. We shook
beneath a screaming sky of hide

and waited without breathing
for death that didn't come.

*Horses*, someone whispered,
*will not tread upon the living.*

*I saw it on the telly.*
*I saw it on the Grand National.*

# Dear Mum

A charge today, we beat them back!
~~It was Bigsy's 18th he died today~~

Am sick of Garibaldis & squeezy cheese!
~~I took out insurance like the sergeant said.~~

Cold here and more sheep than Wales
~~I have trench foot, I may lose some toes.~~

How is Dad how is the dog.
I'm in a hurry. We move off soon.

~~Mummy his brain~~
~~Came out on my hands~~

Serg says we'll be home by my birthday!
Funny that I can fight a war but I can't drink!

Hard to write cos it's very noisy!
~~Mummy I don't think you will know me.~~

~~I tried to hold his head together~~
~~I said it would be all right~~

I've been thinking how bad I used to be.
I'm sorry.

~~Tell Bigsy's mum~~
Your loving son.

# Bruce Lee at Goose Green

We were outnumbered 3 to 1.
We didn't know it of course

until the Argie white flags
popped from the trenches

which was a long time away.
Before then a mine would snap

my arm at the root
& dump it twenty feet away.

I heard someone scream
*I'm only 17 and the bastards*

*have blown off my arm*
and I knew it was me.

The sky was long gone.
In its place was a pyrotechnic display.

My blood shone lovely
as the slow moving streams

of Cumbria where I grew up
& I knew Bruce Lee wouldn't give up.

He'd kill with one arm
twice as many as he did with two.

He'd find a way to get off a minefield –
by leaping, for instance. By leaping

as he did from the walls of my room
every morning of my life.

# Fame!

*I'm going to make it to heaven!*
*Light up the sky like a flame!*

There was a lad from Wales
whose whole village turned out.

I shake hands with the Prince of Wales
and go to the pub straight after.

My mum and dad's mouths hang open
but why are they here who are they to me –

Jimmy and me both feel the same.
We sit in his bedroom drinking all day.

We can't stop laughing.
It's boiling and they're playing

all this crap music in the garden.
I don't really know where I am.

*I'm going to live forever!*
*Baby remember my name!*

\* \* \*

## Bay Tree

I longed for a home.
God gave me someone else's.

I longed to escape my past.
God gave me someone else's.

I longed to be forgiven.
God said, *how can you be?*

*For you know what you do.*
Instead of forgiveness

God gave me a bay tree
that flickers with finches.

I think he means it
to be a lesson.

When the sun rises over my view
I don't know where I am.

I longed to love.
God gave me you.

## You Would Drop Your Spade

There's a god in my head,
quiet, inventive, ambitious,

trying with the unfamiliar
scraps of what's available –

beaches, birches, bungalows,
rubbish, rhodies, retirees –

to recast the shell she occupies
so that you might look up

suddenly from the garden
and see exactly what you lost

coming back to you: a gift
for which faith is not necessary.

You would drop your spade
and cross the garden smiling,

slip your hands into the holes
of this resurrected thing,

kiss it, and know again
the perfect solace of its skin.

# Tour of Landscapes by the Artist

My first:
a father waiting
in an empty tree.
Note his sulky wings,
his shabby stamp
on the sky's gauze.
What is he waiting for,
with no sorrow,
no blink or flap.

My second:
a watercolour teary
as an eye graze.
The sun bent the sky
and I could see lives
magnified from miles away.
All of them I pulled
dripping with light
from the chemical sea.

My latest
(in progress):
a sound piece.
The scowl of a speedboat
undoing the sea.
Note the husband
weeping
in the blaze of the trees.

## Bar Harbor, Maine

Here is where we took the boat
across the harbour whose bed

crawls with lobsters clamouring
*me please! me please!*

who since babyhood
have been thrown back

until the day the familiar hand
closes round a fat blue waist,

and, waving in anticipation,
they land in adult surprise –

here is where we lay side by side
on the pink hotel bed.

Here is where the islands
rose out of the haze,

and you walked the shingle
tracked by a shadow

like a stray that has decided
the future is with you,

scrabbling to catch you,
asking no further questions.

## Shoes

The husband gets home on time.
Each day he is happier, she sees it

like health overwhelming his tired frame,
sweeping away all things unhappy.

On the step she sees her husband's shoes
bent from the happy way he walks.

They point happily towards the house.
No love, no marriage, no fury

nor ecstasy have ever brought
anything of him to her door before.

She watches happily as the shoes
sit patiently in the long evening.

The husband is starting supper
happily in the kitchen.

The wife smiles all the happy evening,
while the shoes wait, warm as dogs.

## Yariguies Brush Finch

> British-led expedition discovers
> new species of bird (October 2006).

You may be dead already,
nipped upright by giant hands,

or perhaps the loll of your head,
beak clamped shut and wings

slammed against escape
simply cry your bewilderment.

I've seen it before: the hunch of the body
when revelations are trawled from the dark,

the body pathetic in its plumage,
flapping a language no one understands.

But without this tiny violence
we will be poorer:

our possession of you
may teach us all we need to know.

Wake little bird. No secret
can resist these gentle hands.

# Marriage

I got married and everything was different.
It seemed impolite to leave, so I didn't.

I began to observe the traces
of my husband, his neatly folded sweaters,

the spaces where he pressed
his life before me.

To touch pictures of him when he was young
made me afraid. I couldn't stop crying,

while my husband brought flowers
and said how sorry he was.

My clothes became too small, as if
they belonged to a sister or a child I'd never had.

Someone said, *you are blooming.*
Of course they could not know

the violence of my marriage.
It broke my heart like a nose.

Its strength shocked me.
Dragged me. Reset me.

## Disorder

My hands are alcoholics
trembling with regret.

My feet are co-dependent,
plodding after the dead,

the frozen, the vanished.
My gut's an obsessive:

I've eaten the same meal
all my life, just like Kafka.

It's the only way I feel
safe, or optimistic at all.

My eyes are bipolar,
seeing too much and not enough;

and of my sectioned ears
only a sliver is visible.

They're ashamed of the pain
that is their life now

and the rabble
they're stuck with

is, with the best will in the world,
fucking up their recovery.

# Farewell My Lovely

> A really good detective never gets married.
> RAYMOND CHANDLER

I'd gotten used to that roomy grin,
the face like a bag of facts,
the flank round as a pony's,
and the way she had of blending in
so badly. But after all,
I didn't really know her,
neither she nor I being the intimate type.

    I take a slug of something
that I've been craving, make a note
of everything that's gone with her.
But my notes become a list
of immovables: this slouching house,
the sea with a face I'd like to smack,
the loosening sky, fit to drop –

    as I'm dusting the mirror
I glimpse her, smart as a rat
in the company of rocks –
but the day's slammed shut
and it's time to file the file.
This is a face to be turned over
for answers from now on.

She's left nothing behind her
to show what was between us.
Always meticulous,
    I find she's slipped
like a last dram into my dreams,
hunched at the scene, wiping fingerprints,
knowing that it's over, that it's time to go.

## Dressed Up As Someone

Last night I dreamed of England,
and I wept in the morning

for my love
of everything gentle.

I wept for the spires
and the meadows

that smiled on me for years
and let me live near them.

I wept for the surly
northern cities

that came, in the end,
to envy me.

Didn't you see me
dressed up as someone

who knows someone?
Didn't you see me

in the beds
of my betters?

Last night I dreamed of England
and I wept in the morning

for the gentle thing
I nearly became,

for the work of art
I was in England.

# Islay

Thirty years ago, I'm sure you lifted
your eyes from her shore, and your gaze
drifted to this rock on the mainland
where I stand remembering you –

as today at the marina, when my husband
glimpsed the *Innisfree*, a boat he knew
long ago. Someone had made her new,
polished the years from her gleaming bow.

He fell silent as she pulled out to sea.
Just like that I think you'd know me now
as if the ocean, the islands, the sun between,
and all we love more had never been.

## Little Black Dog

Take, for instance, the ferns:
one nudge from the sky
and they swirl with all the green
of their first September,

and take the little black dog,
bolting through the scree of sky,
bending and unbending himself
like a letter in determined hands –

he stops at the call of his name
and looks back – he believes the sound,
though the sea convulses
with a universe of names just like it.

The still-green leaves
lie where they were blown,
face down and completely still,
but take, for instance, dying:

the trees are insisting
God doesn't mean it, they insist –
billowing like fabulous ash –
that everything can begin again.

## Dog Opera

…tracking between
rigidity and delight,
never resolving,

so I thought of him as music,
but he was simply waiting
for the moment

that would reveal him,
and one afternoon
she emerged –

her speckled belly
set him moaning:
he fixed on her heels,

his body a god
unfolding in black.
His tongue begged

for a taste of her
as the trees parted,
the mud applauding,

calling them back
and back again
to reveal the finale:

a spotlit clearing,
a dog bowing,
flowers everywhere.

## Trash

Down beside the sour low tide
where Mickey Mouse's yellow hand
drifts across his bursting heart,

the rocks lay out their washed-up wares:
the chins and ears of fancy cups
where grandmas pressed their lips,

the plate's edge I remember
from school, its blue rim
smart and plump as a teapot.

All the teatimes of my childhood
have been smashed here,
and when the tide recedes again

I'm back, pockets stupidly full,
hungry for a time before I knew
I'd be a scavenger of my life.

## Our Baby

shows us that longing
is the matter from which

everything is made,
and when the morning

brims at the window
our baby is fearless.

She faces down
her non-existence,

she regards her would-
be parents kindly.

She watches us endure
the days and nights without her.

Our baby teaches us
to live tenaciously.

In these hard, shining days,
we come to know her.

## Laparoscopy

Doctor Corolla from Egypt
will pump me with $CO_2$,

then slip a camera through
a hole he'll create, and observe.

I will be fast asleep
when Doctor Corolla

ticks off my name,
parts the waves of my gown.

*Slow*, he explains later
when I cling to his cuff.

*But I say six months
you will be pregnant.*

Behind shrunken curtains
the women are weeping

as Doctor Corolla
moves from bed to bed.

*Endometriosis late stage.
Chance of conceiving*

*now 30 percent.
This is what I am telling you.*

A girl smiles thinly from her bed
and I am sick on the kerb.

The sea is nothing to me.
I have a scar, and a promise.

# Moon

It was lost, it did not belong
above this stripped hillside,

the yawn of the estuary,
the chatter of little houses.

It peeped over the hill's shoulder
like an infant, glowing

as the sick do when all else
has failed and God has arrived.

Unable to stop, it rose on,
vast, naked, unable to hide:

the one face we can't forget,
staring back at us from the road.

## Return to Eden

When we were allowed back
we saw the place had changed.

Sea licked its borders,
fish flashed like knives.

Nothing pleased us. Nothing lived up
to what we had suffered to return.

But then, today –
the tiny ghost we see on the screen,

moving inside me without sorrow.
Is it not the shape of everything

before we lost it?
My darling, are we not forgiven?

# Magnificat

Imagine. Your eyes open
onto an angel made of the sea.

Imagine the instruction:
God has chosen you to be

the vessel for his dream.
Instantly the suburbs

become a world of meaning.
The women gather round you,

desperate to touch you.
Imagine. The word *glory*

finally describes the sun
on your geraniums.

You pity your neighbours,
even as they trespass on your lawn.

The butcher stained with blood
is a force for good,

the corner shopkeeper
glows with kindness.

Imagine. You get in your car
and you drive and drive.

Imagine. Nothing in this world
can save you now.

# Beheaded

I hear perfectly: the thud
onto linen, the strange gasp
like the cry of a premature baby,
just once and then silence.

And I see perfectly:
how my lashes scratch the light,
a hair glittering in shadow,
the winded hollow

where my lips rest.
I still have all my words.
I move my mouth,
like someone begging for water.

Fingers grab my hair
and I soar high above my sad
old body, slumped and tiny.
Tears of pity for it fill my eyes.

They are tending it,
the blank women in blue.
They are washing it,
as if they loved it.

Look, the people are cheering me,
look, they are glad to see me,
now that I've been removed
without a single word of protest.

# Special Care Unit

This is where the premature
meet the very old,

dissolving the world's edges
with their soft, accepting sucks.

Each day we cross fifty miles
of broken, birthed earth,

the road twisting into golden fog.
Mountains weep in corners,

are broad-chested and no-nonsense,
and tenderness kicks everywhere:

the practical faces of midwives,
the knife-cleanliness of alcohol,

my husband's hand that was never so strong
until it reached inside an incubator,

and this lonely road,
the canal between darkness and light.

Each night I see my daughter,
my mother, myself,

with tiny, gummy mouth
whispering, *My darling girl,*

*who are you?*
*Have you come to take me home?*

# She

*(after Charles Aznavour)*

She may be a shadow of the past
etched in my body, in my face,
the love that could not hope to last.

She may be the life that's passed,
the road that leaves the faintest trace,
she may be a shadow of the past.

And from her tiny hand is cast
the love that never found a place,
the love could not hope to last

and now is, like youth, surpassed
by her determined, warm embrace.
She may be a shadow of the past.

She may make the night sky vast
and her cries write in empty space
of love that could not hope to last.

In darkened rooms I hold her fast.
I hold her while the planets race.
She may be a shadow of the past,
the love that could not hope to last.

## Ladies

arrive right on time
at your door in the rain

with special equipment
for mulching your brain.

They appear to be women,
they have fluffy names

but they have since undergone
some terrible change.

They growl misinformation
and coo in your phone

*ring us soon Lucy's Mum*
*ring us soon soon soon.*

Women, get a husband
who will say when they've gone

*phew! I'd like a pint*
*of whatever she's on*

and women, keep your husband!
Tend him well, like a border.

Don't let him leave you,
keep your home in good order

or you'll bring them sprinting
in grave disappointment

clipboards glinting
without an appointment.

# Directions

To the left (depending which way
you come) you'll find

a ravenous sea (although
you haven't got the wrong place

if it's furious, or sashaying
in its blue off-the-shoulder).

You'll also see a bus shelter,
and the entrance to School Road.

Keep going. On the right,
a line of old villas, neatly rotting,

and twinkling now it's winter.
Wrapped-up shapes wander in and out

some with children,
some with dogs.

If you come to the Burgh Hall
you've gone too far – turn back

before the rain and wind
make any return impossible.

You've found the house when you see
white gates which will be shut.

A wrapped-up shape
wanders in and out,

sometimes with a baby
sometimes with a dog.

## The First Woman

I became the woman
running out in her slippers

to touch the destroyer
resting at the gate;

I became the woman
who carried her baby

from window to window
like a flare.

I became the woman
weeping on the hour,

who watched *Big Brother*
as minesweepers

gathered on the lawn.
I became the first woman

militarily proven
to disappear.

## Friends

It showed how friendship
doesn't end (like when
Emma and I watched

eight episodes in one go)
though outside my window
the climate was changing

and in my experience
people found each other
quite easy to take or leave.

The day after the last episode
they ran them all again,
protecting me, it seems.

I keep just one from
two-hundred-and-thirty-six.
It's the one where Ross says,

*but this can't be it,*
and Rachel says,
*then how come it is?*

and he sinks to his knees with his arms
around her legs and the camera
moves slowly back

and they hold the shot
for a long time
before the theme tune begins.

# Smile

Sometimes
I forget her

(she's very small
she doesn't speak)

and all that happens
is that she wakes

without me
and she smiles

or cries a little
without me.

It fills my head
on the train

or in my hotel bed
the smile

that comes and goes
without me.

## Another Girl

For I have got
another girl –

another girl –
who will love me till the end.

I don't want to say
I've been unhappy with you

but I have got another girl
who never really went away,

who wakes each day
saying my name,

whose happiness
I promised I would find.

You're making me say
I've got nobody but you

but every promise I made you
I made another girl

and in every dream of you
is another girl.

I don't want to say
I haven't loved you,

'cos it wouldn't be true,
it's just that I have got  *(to fade)*

# The Book of Truths

Under the spreading tree
she pounds the grass,

gives me a long clear
look like a stream

running into the sea.
She squints at the clouds

and smiles; she believes
in them, and in me.

Silently I read to my baby.
Part The First:

Things to Believe
All Your Life –

The earth will not die
and leave you alone.

When the seas overflow,
you will be saved.

Santa, and God,
will watch over you.

I will never disappoint you.
Part the Last:

Don't Read This
Until the Rest no Longer Holds.

Some people, my darling,
some people are just cunts.

# Struck

What made the air ball its fist
and hurl me down?

I didn't curse, simply my wife
surfaced on the crest of pain,

gasping – or was it me
opening and closing my mouth?

I will always remember –
she tried to carry me, and could not.

She pressed her palms to the earth
pronounced it freezing and a terrible distance.

She frowned at the mathematical problem of me
as I dragged my leg like a giant parenthesis.

The air, blowing its knuckles, retreated,
as my wife held me, angel of gas-and-air.

   \* \*

In hospital a woman
inhabited me.

She sat amongst my broken bones
and admonished me.

She was always charming
to busy, evil nurses.

She, too, was undressed for the journey
to the windowless basement

where men in green with speedy names
lean over in masks and exeunt.

Even she at the final second
pointed frantically at medical papers,

and stammered a hope, a wish,
for this or that kindness,

until she was coshed
with technical correctness,

and woke up lashing out
and would not *stop shouting Mr Forrester!*

She moaned in the tunnel of striplights.
She gathered ease, time, cleanliness,

and packed them grimly
like a disappointed wife.

She shut up only when the morphine arrived.
But I knew her, just the same.

\* \*

And though I broke it off cleanly
when my wife arrived with flowers

so that she never knew a thing
and she received me home in sunlight,

the memory came home with me
and occupied the night's bright hours.

In the sunny winter where leaves
drift over the lawn and into the sea,

my wife and I hold hands like newly-weds.
We kiss. We watch films all day.

Our baby squeals at her reflection
which copies her exactly, and soundlessly.

## Baby Group

Save me from my loneliness,
lady of the scar,

lady of the birth trauma
and the absent husband.

Distract me in the rain,
lady of the Asda fairy cake,

vacantly sipping as angels
circle in babywalkers.

And you, lady of perfection,
Boudicca of cashmere

whose baby's shoes are shiny,
whose ribbons reek of adoration,

though we may never say more
than *hello, isn't she lovely!*

I am glad you exist.
You appear on a grey morning

right on time, smart as a sail
on bewildered waters.

## A Bench for Me

To help me sleep
I used to imagine dancing here.

Stupid, I know. After all
it's a hillside above a city.

Highland cows glower
over the fence. Guanacos

dip and flutter beyond.
And everything is tiny

and further away
than you thought.

Here is where I learned
the only lesson that stuck:

that the body is for others
but the face is yours

to press to the breathing side
of something fiercely alive –

the muntjak perhaps
with its flickering skin,

or the macaw, whose feathers
are warm as lips,

covering your eyes softly
as if you were a child.

## Soup

makes me cry.
I find it on my doorstep

with an initial of twigs
on its lid, or in the arms

of a woman who knows
how emptiness lives.

Lentil, chicken, beef.
*Freeze it*, they say.

*Sorry it's not much.*
*I made it today.*

Blessed are the soup-
makers. Blessed

are their feet
that bring them to my door.

Blessed are their hands,
blessed are their eyes

that brim quietly
with all they know.

## Sex in the City

Look at that road
sliced open like a cake,
a cake for me,
surrounded by men
in mucky yellow
their heads thrown back.
I can't take my eyes
off the layers:
the black frosting of tarmac,
its steaming bitumen sauce
then the drool of gravel,
the crunch of hardcore,
and at the very bottom
the men standing knee deep
in a sludge of iron
and laughing, laughing
as if their lovers
had surprised them.

## Last Will and Testament

To Hamish the dog: my blankets, my best rattle, the blocks he chewed.
To my mother: my mattress where my head has made a dip,
                all the photographs.
To my father: his spectacles, which he let me take from his nose and break,
                also my lacy shoes and all my frozen spinach.
To Auntie Jan: the pink cardigan she made me, also my butterfly.
To my mother in addition: my washable nappies (for re-sale), Gina Ford,
                my weaning spoons.
To my father in addition: my words (my *da-da*, my *ba-ba*), my mother,
                my best red trousers.

## Thank You

It was the kind of light
that rocks bend to drink,
and the man in the cowboy hat
with the swans at his feet
braced himself against the gleam.
All the sadness of the hills
was on fire. The swan-galleons
set sail across the grey.
And I ran the length of the loch
to press into your hand this –
for the shining silver of my life.

# Advice to a Daughter

One day you will need help
I cannot give. Certain things

to do with your soul,
which of course is yours alone.

My only advice: one day
someone will cross your path

who spots you're special,
is so convinced in fact

that you become so.
You will probably forget

to thank them, so quietly
did they change your life.

All I can say, darling,
is watch out –

not for the hurts,
they will come and go.

But for those who properly see you.
So that when your life

has turned as it should
you will know to whom it's due.

## To My Husband

This face, this book, this daughter
I commend to you, unfinished.
Read them, darling, and know me.
Keep the rules and the routines:
they will free your nights for dreams,
and in keeping them, you know me.
Stay here, in this old house.
Keep my books on a good shelf
away from the sun, and tell her
what you think I meant.
Learn to cook, and remember how
we ate together, from the day she was born.
Keep the dog off the furniture
until he is old, an old friend of ours,
when it will be time
for you to dress carefully, prepare a speech,
write a letter and leave it unfinished
on our bed – and this daughter,
this face, this book,
you will commend to the future,
finished, beautiful, striding away.

## Tell Laura I Love Her

My father (dead) reaches for the hand
of my mother (now young) and my sister
(long gone) clasps my mother's other hand.

They step together toward the sea.
They're chattering like gods.
How happy they are, my sister

suddenly gathered up
into my mother's arms,
kissed like a diamond.

It's time for me to turn for home
when a voice, a man's voice, says
*You can join them if you want*

and I'm running toward the sea,
my feet pressing into the sand,
brimming with oxygen and blood.

I want to get there, I want to
though my daughter sleeps
and my husband waits

who wouldn't want to
when their father returns
and their mother is young –

is this how it feels
to be forgiven? See –
the immaculate sunset

and their open arms
mouthing for me like a song
that was a hit before I was born.

### EU DECLARATION OF GPSR CONFORMITY

Books published by Bloodaxe Books are identified by the EAN/ISBN printed above our address on the copyright page and manufactured by the printer whose address is noted below. This declaration of conformity is issued under the sole responsibility of the publisher, the object of declaration being each individual book produced in conformity with the relevant EU harmonisation legislation with no known hazards or warnings, and is made on behalf of Bloodaxe Books Ltd on 26 February 2026 by Neil Astley, Managing Director, editor@bloodaxebooks.com.

No part of this book may be used or reproduced in any manner for the purpose of training artificial intelligence technologies or systems. The publisher expressly reserves *Afterlife* from the text and data mining exception in accordance with European Parliament Directive (EU) 2019/790.